The 2,000 Percent Solution Workbook

✦

Practical Questions, Exercises and Suggestions to Create Exponential Performance Gains through Applying the Principles in *The 2,000 Percent Solution*

Donald Mitchell Carol Coles

iUniverse, Inc.

New York Lincoln Shanghai

The 2,000 Percent Solution Workbook
Practical Questions, Exercises and Suggestions to Create Exponential Performance Gains through Applying the Principles in *The 2,000 Percent Solution*

iUniverse books may be ordered through booksellers or by contacting:

iUniverse
2021 Pine Lake Road, Suite 100
Lincoln, NE 68512
www.iuniverse.com
1-800-Authors (1-800-288-4677)

ISBN-13: 978-0-595-37488-5 (pbk)
ISBN-13: 978-0-595-67513-5 (cloth)
ISBN-13: 978-0-595-81881-5 (ebk)
ISBN-10: 0-595-37488-3 (pbk)
ISBN-10: 0-595-67513-1 (cloth)
ISBN-10: 0-595-81881-1 (ebk)

Printed in the United States of America

To our clients, students and colleagues who have helped us understand how to create many more 2,000 percent solutions

Contents

Acknowledgments

The 2,000 Percent Solution Workbook was improved by assistance from many people over a number of years, and space does not permit us to thank each person individually. We hope that each person who contributed will know we appreciate and care about them and are indebted for what they did for this book.

Although we received much assistance, responsibility for any errors or missed opportunities is ours alone.

A few contributors deserve special mention. First, we would like to thank Robert Metz for co-authoring *The 2,000 Percent Solution*. Without his ideas, skill and dedication, that book would have been much less helpful to readers. Second, we would like to thank again all those we acknowledged in *The 2,000 Percent Solution*. This book is based on the concepts in *The 2,000 Percent Solution*, and the strengths of that work are carried into this book. Third, we were greatly assisted in developing these materials through experiences gained in our educational activities with hundreds of CEOs. Thank you for taking time to learn about 2,000 percent solutions and sharing your thoughts about how to create them in your own organizations. Fourth, many of these materials were tested with graduate students in business administration, and we appreciate their sharing with us the 2,000 percent solutions they created. As their solutions became better and better, we knew that we were on the right track with these materials.

Finally, we would like to thank each other for the great support and many contributions each made during the book's development.

The 2,000 Percent Solution Workbook

Introduction

The 2,000 Percent Solution Workbook is intended to serve those who have read *The 2,000 Percent Solution* and are now ready to use or repeat the eight step process described in Part Two of that book for either an existing or a new problem.

The 2,000 Percent Solution was written because Peter Drucker told us that he thought the eight step process we had described to him would solve more than 90 percent of problems that arise inside of organizations. He felt that organizational progress could be greatly accelerated if everyone in an organization learned this process and began using it. He suggested writing a book as the way to begin broader dissemination of the process beyond our client base.

Not knowing what to expect in promoting a new business process, we decided to share what we had learned as broadly as possible. During the launch of *The 2,000 Percent Solution*, we visited over 30 North American cities and conducted learning sessions with hundreds of CEOs located in those cities. While there, we also explained the concept to business journalists. From these activities, we soon noticed that there were better ways of explaining our work than were captured in *The 2,000 Percent Solution*. Since then, we have had the chance to share our work with a broad range of people from around the world, from MBA candidates in countries as far away as Laos to D.B.A. students in Africa to CEOs as near as in our own Boston community. While we helped others learn the 2,000 percent solution process, our ability to communicate that process has improved. *The 2,000 Percent Solution Workbook* greatly benefits from these added perspectives.

While our educational materials and methods have shifted enormously since we wrote *The 2,000 Percent Solution*, we have not previously made those shifts available to all of our readers who are interested in this subject.

To make this workbook easier and more interesting to use, we have avoided duplicating what is in *The 2,000 Percent Solution*. At the same time, we have kept the terminology from that book so that readers of the workbook will not have to learn new meanings or terms.

If you would like to refer back to *The 2,000 Percent Solution* as you use this workbook, please remember that you can find all but two chapters on-line for free at www.2000percentsolution.com (click on the "excerpts" button on the left hand column of the home page, and then select material from the Table of Contents).

A few copies of the original edition of *The 2,000 Percent Solution* (AMACOM Books 1999) can still be found. That edition was supplemented by a reissue edition in 2003 that was available at the time the workbook was initially published in both hard and soft cover from Authors Choice Press. Most on-line sites carry all three versions of *The 2,000 Percent Solution*. The reissue edition can also be ordered through most book stores. In addition, a digital version of the original edition is available from many on-line bookstores including Amazon.com. All references to pagination in *The 2,000 Percent Solution* in this workbook apply to the reissue edition.

Suggested Learning Schedule and Reporting

You will gain the most if you write essays to summarize your learning. The following is an outline of what most people have found to be helpful to them. The suggested schedule assumes that you can devote at least 30 hours a month to this learning.

Month 1: Read *The 2,000 Percent Solution* and take notes on your personal and organizational stalls, potential stallbusters and possible areas for creating a 2,000 percent solution.

Month 2: Read *The 2,000 Percent Solution Workbook* and answer the questions in it.

Month 3: Write four essays.

    a. Describe your personal and organizational stalls (1,000-2,000 words)

    b. Propose two or more stall busters for each stall (2,000-3,000 words)

    c. Describe a 2,000 percent solution you want to create (1,000 words)

    d. Apply the 8-step process to create that solution (3,000-6,000 words)

Month 4: Share your essays with others to obtain comments.

Month 5: Rewrite your essays based on the comments.

Month 6: Begin implementing your solution. Find people who want to learn how to create 2,000 percent solutions

Months 7-11: Mentor those people through the process you used

Month 12: Begin repeating the activities of Months 1-5

PART ONE

What Is a
2,000 Percent Solution?

A 2,000 percent solution is any method of accomplishing what your organization does now in 1/20th the time or less or accomplishing 20 times as much or more, while employing the same or fewer resources. *A combination of those attributes can also be a 2,000 percent solution.*

Technology often helps us speed results without increasing resources. For example, you can send material halfway around the world now in an e-mail for a tiny fraction of the cost and time of sending an air courier package. The e-mail is a 2,000 percent solution compared to the best method available 20 years ago, sending a facsimile.

Thinking more clearly about the implications of what needs to be done can have a similar effect without waiting for technology to advance. For instance, many electronic products are now designed to have many fewer parts than the products they replace. Consequently, repairing products with fewer parts takes much less time and costs less. For more expensive products, the parts are often monitored electronically to note when they are about to fail. The message that failure is imminent is sent to the repair person before the failure. The part is replaced, and the customer never experiences a problem. Repeat sales and profits improve as a result. For less expensive products, on-line resources allow customers to diagnose their problems, implement their own solutions and receive faster results at a fraction of the cost for providing hands-on repairs.

Sharing information throughout organizations has had similar effects. Many organizations now use business intelligence software that allows everyone to know what performance is in activities that each person influences. As a result, fewer problems occur and the solutions come faster and less expensively.

In this part of the workbook, we will look at why 2,000 percent solutions are available for just about any activity and how to overcome organizational and personal stalls (ineffective, unthinking habits) that keep 2,000 percent solutions at bay.

Chapter 1

2,000 Percent Solutions Are Available for Almost Any Activity

The material in this chapter expands upon pages 1-6 in *The 2,000 Percent Solution*.

A corollary to Pareto's Law (referred to by many as the 80/20 principle, meaning that 80 percent of the results can be observed to come from 20 percent of the people doing an activity) states that 80 percent of the results of any economic activity come from 20 percent or fewer of the efforts. By examining an example of this corollary, the naturally high frequency of 2,000 percent solutions can be better understood.

Imagine that a business has 100 salespeople. Consistent with Pareto's Law, 20 of those salespeople produce total sales of 80,000 units per year while the remaining 80 salespeople produce total sales of only 20,000 units per year. The most productive 20 salespeople average 4,000 units per year while the 80 less productive average sales of 250 units per year. The 20 most productive salespeople create 16 times (4,000/250) the results of the average of the 80 remaining sales people. Thus, just matching what the most productive 20 salespeople accomplish is a 1,600 percent solution.

Within the group of 20, some are more productive than the others. Let's assume that the most productive salesperson produces annual sales of 7,000 units. That amount is 28 times what the 80 less productive salespeople average. If the less productive people can move up to the productivity of the most productive salesperson, that's a 2,800 percent solution.

Within the group of 80, some are less productive than others. Let's assume that the least productive salesperson who won't be fired sells merely 100 units per year. If that person could match the most productive salesperson, that would be a 7,000 percent solution.

The nature of which customers are served may have something to do with why the two salespeople vary so much in productivity. But if the least productive salesperson can increase performance to half that of the average of the most productive group, that's still a 2,000 percent solution

Let's also assume that the company has a more effective competitor where the most productive salespeople average selling 10,000 units per year. Within that group, let's also assume that the most productive person sells 18,000 units per year. If some of this success is based on selling methods that the least productive salesperson in the first company can emulate, that relatively low performing salesperson would only have to capture 1/9 of the results of this most productive competitor's salesperson to achieve a 2,000 percent solution.

In addition, there are probably better performing salespeople in other industries who could also inform the lowest producing salesperson in the original company how to improve.

From the first company's management perspective, notice that the problem is different. Only if all the salespeople in total improve their productivity by 20 times does the company enjoy a 2,000 percent solution. If the methods and personal qualities of the best few salespeople can be duplicated in the rest of the sales force, such a 2,000 percent solution can be achieved.

Pareto's Law also applies to every other activity that a person does in a company: Twenty percent of the employees will produce eighty percent of the results. By learning from the best inside and outside the company, the most productive employees can improve further. Likewise, twenty percent of the customers will produce 80 percent of the earnings. So it's important who you sell to and help as well as how efficiently you perform. Many organizations will find that their most effective salespeople are mostly bringing in business from relatively unprofitable customers. As a result the best practice may be found among a so-called average performer who only produces high margin sales. Cross-fertilize the methods of the high volume salesperson with the high-margin one, and you should increase the profit-productivity of sales efforts by much more than 2,000 percent.

For a given organization, simply measuring to find out who is the most productive and what they do differently that may account for their success can be a very powerful tool for helping others to expand their effectiveness. That's why the few companies that do such benchmarking within a company are quick to find ways to make enormous improvements in their effectiveness.

At Mitchell and Company, we measured a large number of companies that did the same activities to see how their effectiveness compared to others. Much like what Pareto's Law suggests, companies were highly effective compared to other firms in only a few areas...usually fewer than 5 percent of their important functions. Companies were about as effective as the average firm in about 30% of their important activities. And these same companies were well below average in the remaining activities.

That measurement made us realize the enormous potential of outsourcing. If you have some activity where you are well below average throughout your company, you may have the potential for a 2,000 percent solution by simply outsourcing that same activity to a top performing outside organization.

We all know that each activity varies in its significance. For instance, developing new medicines at a pharmaceutical company is much more valuable than most other activities. If your company is below average in such an important activity, the company-wide benefits of either improving to become above average or outsourcing to an organization that is above average can be a 2,000 percent solution for the entire company's profits. As a result, those who are wise in selecting the activities to improve first can make much faster progress than those who focus in less significant activities.

Further, you should consider that some companies are making it a priority to develop skill in developing and implementing 2,000 percent solutions among as many people as possible. Such organizations will have vast advantages over those who simply look at the internal best practice, the industry best practice or outsource to a highly effective outside organization. Such companies will be able, instead, to advance beyond the future best practice towards the theoretical best practice. Implementing beyond the future best practice usually creates at least 5,000 percent solutions. Coming close to a theoretical best practice often creates 10,000 percent solutions. If you create a 2,000 percent solution that also serves to greatly expand the market by adding new users of your offerings, the gains can be an exponential factor larger.

From that perspective, you can see that achieving a 2,000 percent solution is often a modest target...even though at first blush it would seem to be the opposite, a stretch goal. Clients and students who have worked on creating 2,000 percent solutions were often able to reach 20 times higher performance levels within 6 months of implementing this process. Rarely does it take longer than two years to stimulate performance to these higher levels. Individuals who are developing 2,000 percent solutions usually report being able to create the plan for one with less than 60 hours of effort over a few weeks.

Questions to Help You Create 2,000 Percent Solutions

Now, let's look at some questions to help you get started in achieving similar results. Since this is a workbook, we suggest that you jot down your answers in the spaces provided. These notes will be helpful to you when you repeat the eight step process in the future by reminding you of what you did and did not consider.

1. What activities in your organization have the most positive impact on total profits *now*?

For a mining company, the answer may be reducing the cost of raw materials by extracting the lowest cost ore first. For a manufacturing company, the answer may lie in avoiding costly errors in its products so that rework and warranty costs are avoided. For a wholesaler, the answer may lie in purchasing the lowest cost items and being able to keep those goods in stock with low inventory levels. For a brokerage firm, it may be interesting clients in trading more frequently in profitable ways for the clients and the firm.

2. What activities in your organization will have the most impact on total profits *five years from now?*

For the mining company, the answer may be locating new sources of lower cost ore. For the manufacturing company, the answer may lie in redesigning products and developing new products that are less expensive to make and cause fewer errors in producing. For the wholesaler, the answer may lie in creating new computer systems that allow for more efficient purchasing and management of inventory. For a brokerage firm, it may be adding new services and increasing the value of existing services to attract more profitable clients and retain them longer.

3. In which of these activities do you suspect that some of your organization's efforts are much more productive than the least effective efforts?

Although you cannot know until you measure, you have probably observed differences in performance or heard stories that lead you to believe that there are differences in some areas. These differences may occur from individual to individual (such as how rapidly and correctly transactions are processed), office to office among people doing the same function (such as regional sales and administrative operations), or from plant to plant producing the same item.

4. What measurements already exist that could help you identify the size and value of these differences in performance?

In many cases, measurements are not available in a convenient form for this purpose, but could be assembled to help you understand differences. For example, you may have individual productivity by employee in some performance areas. Those individual data could be combined to determine if office by office productivity differs. That measurement would be helpful because it could help identify superior management practices in some locations that are not performed in other locations. Many people assume that such measurements only exist in accounting, information technology and manufacturing functions. Be sure to also ask people who work in the activities that interest you. You may be pleasantly surprised to find out that there are other measurements in place that you have never seen.

5. What measurements could you inexpensively add for other high value opportunities where you have no information about relative performance now?

Talk with those who would have to be involved in making the new measurements to learn their ideas about what can be done easily and inexpensively. Then, take a little time to make these measurements on a one-time basis. Later you can decide if it is worth continuing these new measurements.

6. What do the measurements you have already suggest the greatest differences in the value of performance are?

In looking at this question, you should be sure to consider the economic impact of differences in performance as well as the percentage size of the differences in performance. For example, your most productive salesperson may be selling 50 times as much as the least productive. But if everyone operated at that level, you might only save one percent of revenues. If everyone matched your most productive design engineer in finding less costly and more valuable ways to redesign existing products and design new ones, you might save as much as five percent of revenues. Obviously, the latter alternative would be the one to work on first assuming that all else is equal.

7. Where do you suspect that the greatest value differences in performance are among areas where you have no measurements available?

8. How hard will it be to make improvements in performance in the most valuable opportunity activities identified in questions 6 and 7?

In answering this question, you need to consider difficulty, risk of not succeeding, cost of working on the problem compared to what you can afford and how long you can expect it to take in the worst case. Many such changes are difficult. The most challenging are those performance areas where people have to change their long-held habits and beliefs. Don't rely solely on your own judgment in answering this question. Speak with those who work in those areas as well as outside experts who have helped organizations improve performance in these areas.

9. What area of performance improvement should be your top priority?

Our suggestion is that you pick an area with a high payoff which can probably be improved rapidly with fewer resources and risk than other activities you are considering. Be sure to consider the potential enthusiasm with which those who will need to change will probably view the necessary adjustments. If in doubt, pick the activity where enthusiasm is highest for the needed changes.

Chapter 2

Remove Stalls that Block 2,000 Percent Solutions

The material in this chapter expands upon pages 7-127 in *The 2,000 Percent Solution*.

Stalls are unconsidered habits that impede an organization's progress. Habits, good and bad, are formed by our response to stimuli. When these habits are repeated often enough, there is little conscious thought before we act in the habitual ways. Usually, such habits once served a positive purpose. For example, many companies began improving their quality by double-checking their work. If the way of working changed since then so that errors are automatically elimi-nated, many people will continue to double-check the work. Why? Well, they will feel very uneasy if they don't. It's almost like a superstition at that point. In many cases, conscientious workers will keep double-checking the work even if they are ordered not to do so.

In *The 2,000 Percent Solution*, we looked at a handful of the most common organizational stalls. These stalls involved tradition (chapter 2), disbelief (chapter 3), misconceptions (chapter 4), being repelled by unattractiveness (chapter 5), poor communications (chapter 6), bureaucracy (chapter 7), and procrastination (chapter 8). What all of these stalls have in common is that are based in a compla-cent attitude that seldom questions whether something needs to be improved and how such improvement might be accomplished.

Since we wrote *The 2,000 Percent Solution*, many CEOs have helped us to appreciate stalls that are often specific to their company roles. Perhaps the worst one these CEOs identified is the "you need to check with me" stall. Some CEOs require that every little step be checked. Since there's only one person who is CEO, progress on all fronts is delayed while capable people wait for the go-ahead. Soon, initiative is sapped and even the most inventive are likely to lose a lot of their curiosity and drive. Yet many CEOs pride themselves on this approach, feel-ing that it eliminates bureaucracy. While such organizations have avoided some bureaucracy, an overly directive and busy CEO can be a worse stall than any bureaucracy you can imagine in a relatively small company.

Some people have concluded that there are relatively few stalls that you need to be on the look-out for. That conclusion seems to be unwarranted. Our clients and readers keep pointing out new stalls to us. For example, many people have reported that so-called experts are given too much influence in many situations. The expert may not know all of the facts, may assume too much, and the expertise may not be relevant for the task at hand. Blindly following the expert's directions can lead to serious problems in those circumstances. A well-known example is that engineers are often intrigued by the potential to use fewer resources in daring ways to create "elegant" solutions. In creating those solutions, they may ignore conditions that will predictably occur every so often. In the early days of building large suspension bridges, for example, a number of such elegant, dainty bridges disintegrated because they could not bear high wind speeds buffeting them from unusual directions. Likewise, the newer John Hancock Tower in Boston for a number of years was a source of broken glass shards for blocks around as its beautiful glass panes shattered with little advance notice in high winds.

What you can count on is that your organization will have different stalls than its competitors and most of your suppliers and customers. You should probably also assume that you have some stalls for which no name has yet been applied. How can you be sure that you have identified your most important stalls? In this activity, there are no guarantees...but we do have some suggestions.

First, you will find many of the stalls we have identified in either *The 2,000 Percent Solution* or *The Irresistible Growth Enterprise* (Stylus, 2000), which looks at stalls associated with failing to be flexible in adapting to irresistible forces outside your control. Further, we have identified a stall in sticking with current business models in *The Ultimate Competitive Advantage* (Berrett-Koehler 2003). Be sure to check for the signs of the stalls that are described in those books.

Second, we occasionally add new stalls to our www.2000percentsolution.com Web site that have been suggested by our readers. Check in there once in awhile to see what's new on this front.

Third, use the questions in this chapter to help you search out current and potential stalls that you cannot recognize from looking at the sources listed above.

Fourth, introduce others in your organization to the important art of identifying and overcoming stalls. Many stalls that are invisible to you will be very plain to them. For instance, in many companies order processes that require only 2-3 hours of total effort stretch out to last for weeks because so many people have to deal with parts of the process in an unvarying order. Such delays are often invisible to management but apparent to customers and those who work in the process.

Fifth, assume that efforts you have put into place to overcome stalls will fail to work as well after awhile. Go back and see how you are doing on a frequent basis and be prepared to identify and apply new stall busting methods.

As you follow this advice, begin by only looking at the performance area you identified in answering question 9 in chapter one.

Questions to help your organization identify and overcome stalls that are reducing your performance.

You will be more successful in this activity if you prepare yourself. If you are not familiar with all of the current steps involved in the performance area or activity you want to improve, be sure to take the time to observe and participate in that performance area so your thinking is influenced by the facts rather than by opinions or out-of-date information. If possible, have those who work in the area share their observations independently of your own thinking. In addition, check your answers with those who are involved in the performance area.

1. What are the causes of avoidable delays?

A good way to begin is to assume that you are personally going to do all of the steps involved in the performance area or activity you want to improve. Then, find the resources, knowledge, skill and information to do that work in the fastest, most effective way. After you have identified how you would do the activity yourself with the right resources, see what current delays can be eliminated. Then, determine what would have to change in order to eliminate those delays.

Here's an example. Let's look at the sales process of finding and attracting a new customer. Many organizations provide leads to help sales people focus their initial contacts. In some organizations, these leads are only provided every month or so. In between, the sales people can follow up on old leads...but have no new ones to focus on. Changing the lead generation process to provide leads more often would allow salespeople the ability to make new contacts daily. In addition, if the leads are received more often, the leads are probably based on more recent expressions of interest by potential customers. Sales results are bound to improve in such a circumstance. If the lead generation source is already adding leads daily, all that has to change is to transmit those leads daily to your company rather than less frequently. In many cases, the cost of doing so will be lower because a report may be eliminated in the process change.

2. Why haven't the avoidable delays been eliminated in the past?

You need to know the historical reason for the delays continuing because otherwise you won't know how to address the change process.

In some cases, the source of a delay may relate to some existing process that has not been changed recently. In those instances, the delay may simply be a function of no one having looked lately at how to make faster progress. In other cases, your computer systems may be the source of the delay, and no one wants to put in the time and effort to change them except for a very good reason. Elsewhere, you may find that there are differences of opinion about what should be done, and no one wants to take on the political challenges of advocating and leading a change. In some other circumstances, you may find that the delay is actually a defense mechanism that some people use to diffuse pressure for higher performance. Be sure to keep looking until you find some unconscious habits that are reinforcing the continued delays.

3. How will customers, employees, suppliers, distributors, partners, shareholders, lenders and the communities you serve be affected by eliminating the delays?

You will find that solutions which obviously benefit each stakeholder will be those that will be easiest to implement. If eliminating delays is harmful to some of these stockholder groups while being positive for others, rethink the subject to consider how the delays could be eliminated so that everyone would benefit. In some cases, that may mean providing some of the economic benefit of the change to those who will be somewhat harmed by it to more than offset any harm.

4. Are there ways of eliminating delays that help with more than one kind of delay?

Most organizations have a limited capacity for change that is always being exceeded. In such circumstances, people may just spin their wheels and feel frustrated. If you can find ways to eliminate the delays that require fewer or easier changes, you will be more likely to succeed in this and other important initiatives that the organization is pursuing.

5. What could go wrong when you eliminate delays?

Productivity often falls when an organization puts in a productivity improving change. A common reason for such a perverse result is that not enough preparation has been done so that everyone knows what he or she needs to do. With time, appropriate learning usually develops and results improve. But with careful thinking in advance about the downside risk, you can often eliminate these painful, temporary setbacks that sap enthusiasm for the new direction.

6. What are the least demanding ways to avoid the delays?

As you know from *The 2,000 Percent Solution*, great progress occurs each time you repeat the eight step process. If you pursue these changes in less demanding ways, you will finish putting this 2,000 percent solution into practice sooner so that you can begin repeating the process faster as well.

7. What other benefits will you gain from making these changes?

When you aim to make a 2,000 percent solution, you often will make improvements in other activities and areas that you were not considering. As you begin to focus on creating a 2,000 percent solution in the next part of the workbook, the perspectives you gain from this question will help point you in the most effective direction.

PART TWO

Choose a 2,000 Percent Opportunity

In Part One of the workbook, you looked for high payoff areas and activities to create 2,000 percent solutions and the stalls you would have to overcome in the process of making improvements. Those perspectives will have narrowed down your thinking quite a lot. In Part Two, you will find opportunities that will increase performance in a large number of areas and think about how long it will take to make the improvements required for one 2,000 percent solution versus the time needed for another one. At the end of Part Two, you will be ready to begin crafting a 2,000 percent solution.

Let's consider an example of how the choice of creating a 2,000 percent solution can make a large positive or negative difference for an organization. In earlier days at Apple Computer, the organization set its focus on having a superior operating system and user features that would make it very appealing to do advanced computing on an Apple Macintosh. For many years after the IBM PC standard was set, users consistently reported preferences for Apple's offerings. The only aspect where the PC standard did well compared to Apple was in having more application software available for PCs. Microsoft was a much smaller company at the same time, and also had an objective of providing a superior operating system for personal computers. Microsoft focused its attention solely on improving its software and the frequency of upgrades in creating its 2,000 percent solutions for its computer users. Apple continued to work across the board on all aspects of computing that affected its hardware or software. If Apple instead had selected the Microsoft focus, Apple could have chosen to make its proprietary operating system work on the PC standard as well. Microsoft would have continued to do well on IBM-built personal computers, but Apple could have gained leadership with most of the clone PC makers who soon dominated the market. If successful in that focus, Apple would now be the world's most valuable company and would probably have stopped providing its own computing hardware at some point along the way.

As you can see from this example, it's important to think about the benefits that current customers and stakeholders receive. But it's even more important to think about the benefits that potential stakeholders will obtain as well. In addition, how will your change affect the competitive balance in the market place? Can you, like Apple might have, cut off a powerful future competitor by concentrating your focus where it will do you the most good?

Chapter 3

Select Opportunities that Help Performance in Many Areas

The material in this chapter expands upon pages 200-205 in *The Irresistible Growth Enterprise*.

In *The Irresistible Growth Enterprise*, we describe a strategic thinking method that can help you address where focus will do you the most good compared to competitors and in absolute success. In that book, we talk about nth degree thinking. That process requires you to take one element of your business environment and expand it to extremes…both much larger and much smaller than you can possibly imagine could occur. That stretching out makes it easier to see where making an adjustment relative to irresistible forces can make a useful difference, regardless of what happens with irresistible forces.

In picking 2,000 percent solution opportunities, you also apply nth degree thinking. To do so you stretch the benefits that stakeholders could gain or lose to their limits, rather than stretching the irresistible forces.

Here's an example. Linear Technology specializes in providing semiconductors that allow portable electronic devices to operate longer on battery power. If we look at that battery-life-extending quality, stretching the benefit to the nth degree means having portable devices that never lose power while you are using them. Under such circumstances, we could expect that every device that is now used in a plugged-in, stationery environment would be more often supplemented by a portable version…assuming weight and other forms of inconvenience did not prohibit that use. For a comparison, Linear Technology could also look at the effect of vastly lowering the costs to provide its semiconductors and how much that would change benefits to customers and ultimate consumers. Since these chips are a small part of the portable devices and Linear Technology has a high market share, this cost benefit is probably smaller than by making battery life unlimited. In that is the case, Linear Technology should focus on its battery-life-extending qualities rather than cost reductions.

In looking at the technical limits of its semiconductors to extend battery life, Linear Technology needs to then apply the nth degree thinking to the various technical choices to accomplish unlimited battery life. These choices might include using less power to perform the same task, draining batteries less for the same power usage and gaining more stored energy through the device's use. If any of these qualities could be extended to the nth degree, that quality would enable unlimited device use.

The nth degree test next needs to be applied to the theoretical limits of each technology choice. For instance, if a device were operated with only the minimum power required by current technology, how much could power usage be reduced? If batteries were drained in the optimal way, how much longer would they last? If more energy could be stored through the device's use through solar panels and heat exchanges, how much would that extend battery life? Without going into the physics of the problem, let's assume for our purposes that storing more energy is the maximum improvement that is theoretically available. After all, devices are usually located in warm environments with lots of light around, held by people in even warmer hands, moved and poked at with fingers, and taken into different physical environments. Which technical solutions would work best at the lowest cost? Those potential solutions should become the focus of finding one change that will create the most benefits.

If you do not work in a high technology environment, you may be wondering what your choices might look like. Let's consider a book publisher. Assume that our book publisher examines the following areas using the nth degree test for competitive and profit impact: cost of development; cost of production; duration of development; distribution availability in bookstores; amount of publicity; amount of positive word-of-mouth comments; pleasure that readers get from the book; what percentage of readers like the book; and pricing. Notice that taking the number of positive word-of-mouth comments to the maximum would tend to overwhelm the other areas. Most publishers, however, don't put much attention in that area. A publisher that did could probably expect to create an overwhelming 2,000 percent solution for its books and its publishing performance.

Questions to help your organization identify the area where performance improvement will create the greatest benefits.

In thinking about finding the greatest benefits, it's good to keep two time frames in mind. The first is for the effects in one year of less. The second is for the effects in five years or more. The reason for keeping these two time periods in mind is because customer preferences are always shifting from one direction into another. The benefit you choose to emphasize should be one that will have immediate, substantial benefits while providing even larger, more important benefits over the longer term.

1. What benefits could your products or services provide to customers and ultimate users?

It's important to think about both what benefits you could provide today and those potential benefits that you could deliver later. At this stage, the longer your list is the better your eventual results will probably be. Don't rule anything out for now. Later steps in the workbook will help you sort out areas that aren't promising for all possible reasons. So for now, open your mind as wide as you can. This process will work best if you apply this thinking to one customer, product or service at a time.

2. If the positive side of each benefit was expanded as large as possible, which benefit would be most valuable in stimulating purchases from your organization?

Although many people will want to apply maximum rigor in answering a question like this, it usually turns out that common sense can provide an equally valid answer with much less time and effort. If you find that several benefits seem to share the lead in providing maximum value, simply continue to focus on all of those benefits in the remainder of this chapter's questions.

3. How might you take that most potentially valuable benefit to the maximum?

A good brainstorming session is called for here. Gather around people from a variety of backgrounds (including a number that are unrelated to what you do). Describe the benefit that you want to take to the nth degree, and ask each person to describe as many ways as possible that the nth degree might be reached. As before, place no limits on ideas.

4. In looking at potential solutions to take the potentially most valuable benefit to the maximum that you defined in 3 above, which solution alternatives would also drive other highly valuable benefits forward?

Here, you are trying to find overlap where a potential solution provides enhanced effectiveness that helps more than one highly valuable benefit when provided to the nth degree.

5. Which of the potential solutions that advances many benefits towards the nth degree would be the easiest for your organization to implement?

In considering your choices, be sure to include your ability to access the talents of other organizations through partnering, outsourcing and other potential relationships.

Chapter 4

Consider How Long It May Take to Create a 2,000 Percent Solution

The material in this chapter does not relate to any specific section in *The 2,000 Percent Solution*.

In chapter 3, you identified some potential solutions that work well with your organization's capabilities to create nth degree advances in a number of customer and end user benefits that would create enormous increases in your sales. Now, it's time to examine those potential solutions for how long it will take to make progress.

Time is an important element in focusing your attention because benefits that arrive sooner are surer and more valuable than ones that take longer. Certainly, in choosing between creating a 2,000 percent solution that you can put in place over a few months and one that will require decades, most would choose to pursue first the one that requires only months. An analysis of the present value of the cash flow benefits would also validate that choice.

Let's pick up on the publishing example from chapter 3 to look at the time implications of the choices facing the publisher. The publisher's most valuable benefit for increased sales is to generate unlimited amounts of positive word of mouth about its books.

Here are some of the potential solutions that the publisher might have identified that help improve other benefits:

— Publish books written by well-regarded celebrities with intriguing new information

— Authors dedicate royalties to popular charities which will promote the books

— Companies donate books as part of their product promotions due to the subject matter

— Tie the book launch timing to a series of related broad-scale media events

– Create an appealing corporate-sponsored contest related to the theme of the book

–Provide newsworthy disclosures daily related to the book.

Next, the publisher needs to think about how long it would take to pursue each of these potential solutions. Clearly, there are only a limited number of celebrities who could have the right kind of appeal and would be willing to tailor their books to this purpose and donate their proceeds to charity. One might work on attracting those celebrities forever, and still not gather a single one. Some other approach for adding word-of-mouth interest is needed. This conclusion is particularly true for a small publisher whose market strengths might not be considered to be valuable enough to attract such celebrities.

Many celebrities are already associated with corporations through endorsement contracts and charities through voluntary activities. Having identified which celebrities the publisher wants to pursue, the next step is to research their commitments and connections to corporations and charities. Then, the publisher could see which celebrities could be approached through these intermediaries. The best starting point would probably be a charity. In some cases, the publisher might find that the corporate sponsor and the charity also have a tie. That combination could be even better.

As the publisher, you next need to develop a book concept that fits with all of these circumstances. Then, you should document why the book concept will be very valuable to the celebrity, the charity and the corporate sponsors.

How long would it take to pursue these activities? Not very long if you know what needs to be done, but most publishers don't have the skills in house to advance such an approach into reality. Currently, publishers wait for authors' agents to approach them with such packages...and then the acquisition editors choose among the proposals for the most valuable book concepts.

What's required is not unlike what theatrical, motion picture and television producers do. An important step might be to develop a partnership with such a producing organization that could participate in providing some of the other entertainment that could be built around the concept. Our publisher needs to focus attention on either working with people who have these skills and contacts or hiring such people.

No one should build a possible route towards a 2,000 percent solution around one potential set of allies. So our publisher needs to explore associations with other potentially enabling parties, like the celebrities' agents, corporations and nonprofit organizations that sponsor popular events, and entertainment impresarios. Another approach might involve partnering with foundations that wanted to help pioneer this type of nonprofit fund-raising. Such foundations could use their own contacts to help put the necessary talent and skills together.

The publisher should continue to focus on potential solutions until several paths have been found that can be fairly quickly explored and implemented. At that point the publisher will be ready to begin developing a 2,000 percent solution using the materials and questions in the next eight chapters of this workbook.

If the publisher cannot find several paths for word-of-mouth increases that seem to have high potential, the publisher would be wise to shift focus. That publisher should look instead for rapid paths for pursuing some of the other benefits that the nth degree analysis identified as being particularly valuable in chapter 3, such as pleasure that readers get from the book and, how many readers like the book which can help build positive word-of-mouth-based interest.

Questions to help your organization identify the opportunities for 2,000 percent solutions that can be implemented most rapidly.

As the publishing example showed, there can be many pathways to creating a 2,000 percent solution that improves a high profile benefit while enhancing many other benefits as well. With these questions, you will identify the opportunities that you want to use the eight-step process to develop.

1. If you had unlimited resources and skills, how would you create the most immediate and valuable benefits for your customers and end users?

Since no organization has unlimited resources and skills, this may sound like a hypothetical question. Our experience has been that there are usually ways of approaching the level of unlimited resources and skills by joining with other organizations and individuals whose positions are complementary to your own. By addressing "what" needs to be accomplished, then it becomes easier to consider "who" you need to work with to get the results you seek.

2. What resources and skills do you lack now to implement those ideas?

Make as extensive a list as you can to identify what is missing so that you can separately focus on how to fill in each gap.

3. How can you eliminate these resource and skill weaknesses through adding information and knowledge?

Your choices include hiring people who already are well informed and knowledgeable, helping those who work for you to add the information and knowledge that they are missing and involving suppliers and potential partners.

4. Which organizations are in the best position to implement the ideas you have for your organization?

Naturally, if you can access all the resources and skills from a few (or even one) organizations, there will be faster progress towards your goal. Otherwise, coordination with too large a group of other organizations can make implementation unusually difficult.

5. How can you interest those organizations in working with you, rather than one of your competitors?

This is an area where imagination helps. Organizations that are more capable than yours are already quite busy pursuing opportunities in which they do not need to share the rewards. Your opportunity needs to put some of their current opportunities to shame by comparison, even after you reap your expected reward from the new success. Obviously, this change in priorities is easier to do when the other organization is smaller than yours. The best opportunities for you, however, will probably require help from those who are much larger than you are. How can you make that organization's involvement be simple, easy and enormously attractive?

In *The Ultimate Competitive Advantage* (Berrett-Koehler 2003), we outline a case history of how Goldcorp engaged most of the best mining geologists in the world to help identify Goldcorp's best exploration possibilities. See pages 23-27. This example is also explained in chapter 11 of this workbook. How could you pursue a similar approach to add the resources and skills you need?

6. Which methods of acquiring the necessary resources and skills are most likely to succeed?

If it seems unlikely that you can overcome the obstacles to develop your 2,000 percent solution with some methods, you would be better off to focus on the methods where you now think you see your way clear to the solution.

7. How long will each of these more certain methods take?

In thinking about this question, assume that you will experience the usual setbacks that occur when any organization does something for the first time.

8. Including the time to acquire the resources and skills you need, which five ways of providing the most immediate and valuable benefits for your customers and end users can you probably complete first? Identify how long you think the total elapsed time will be.

PART THREE

Apply the Stall Buster's Guide in Eight Steps

In using this part of the workbook, we suggest that you focus your attention throughout the next eight chapters on the opportunity you identified in chapter three of the workbook to create large amounts of benefit for your customers and end users. You should also plan to explore the five best ways of acquiring the resources and skills you need to be successful that you spelled out in chapter four.

The biggest mistake people make when first working on 2,000 percent solutions is to select opportunities that offer limited benefits from a 2,000 percent solution. As an extreme example of this, one CEO told us that he wanted to work first on improving his compensation system. A far better choice would have been to improve some aspect of performance and to begin on the compensation system as part of step seven of the eight step process.

A 2,000 percent solution requires following all of the eight steps outlined in part two of *The 2,000 Percent Solution* in the order described there.

As you answer the questions in this workbook, you may find yourself wanting to have a little more background on a particular step. We encourage you to reread the relevant section in *The 2,000 Percent Solution*. The eight step process begins with chapter 9 and continues through chapter 16 in that book.

Since you will repeat answering the questions in this part, we suggest that you be sure to keep your completed workbook. In future repetitions of the process, you will benefit from rereading your earlier answers. To preserve this opportunity for repetitions past the first one, you should also plan to keep your notes on how you answer these questions in the future as well.

As you pursue these eight chapters, you will find a shift in focus from *The 2,000 Percent Solution* in some parts of the eight step process. We have made these modifications to reflect what has worked best for our clients and students since we wrote the book back in 1998. We hope you will find these adjustments to be helpful to you as well.

Chapter 5

Step One: Understand the Importance of Measuring Performance

The material in this chapter expands upon pages 129-148 in *The 2,000 Percent Solution*.

Many people are surprised when they rapidly find many innovative ideas for creating breakthrough progress by using the questions in Part One. Two factors contribute to this enhanced creativity. First, you have used the questions in the workbook to explore areas of potential that you probably have not fully considered before. Second, by thinking about the opportunity in more detail and assuming that you could have unlimited resources and skills, you opened your mind to new areas of implementing improvements that you had not thought about before.

Let's now turn that successful experience into lessons about the value of measurements. Move back in time and consider what measurements you could have put into place that would have revealed the opportunities you are now considering sooner…even without this workbook.

If you are like most people, you will discover that you haven't been measuring the nth degree potential of opportunities to expand profitable demand from customers and end users. Instead, you have probably focused your measurements on how effective you are in serving customers and end users by doing what you already do. You need both sets of measurements to succeed. The nth degree measurements tell you "what" you should be emphasizing and the measurements of how you are performing now tell you "how" you are doing in pursuing the best "what" area.

The nth degree measurement gap can easily be filled by using a combination of survey techniques, detailed examinations of your most developed markets and market tests involving vastly changed benefits for customers and end users. We strongly encourage you to begin working with skilled practitioners to put the necessary nth degree measurements in place.

Most people discover from their new nth degree measurements is that they are totally unaware of some of the best ways to create more profitable near-term demand for your offerings. You are highly likely to find an even better opportunity than any of the ones you identified in chapter 3. As a result, it's very important that you develop nth degree measurements before you repeat the eight step process in considering the opportunity you selected based on chapter 3.

These nth degree measurements can bring you an unexpected benefit: New insights into how to move faster and less expensively to nth degree effectiveness. For instance, the publishing company in the example developed in chapters 3 and 4 could use such measurements to identify which celebrities, which new information, which charities, which sponsors, which media events, what kind of a contest and what daily disclosures would work best to work with. A company that already had such information could then be much more precise and effective in finding the fastest, easiest ways to implement those insights.

Naturally, you should also examine why your organization doesn't already have nth degree elasticity measurements in place. The source of that lack will uncover stalls that are holding your organization back in other ways as well as denying you these measurements. For many organizations, the root cause will be an over focus on "meeting budget." In such organizations, anything that doesn't contribute to meeting this year's or next year's budget is looked at as being entirely optional. But that short-term focus can paradoxically cause an organization to miss its best opportunities to prosper this year and next. It's like a runner only developing conditioning to run for a short period of time. That runner will be failing to reach his or her full potential. With different conditioning, much faster times over longer courses would soon follow.

Another helpful focus for your new nth degree measurements is to search for the potential achievements of the people and organizations with whom you seek to partner. For example, how can they derive the most benefit out of the new directions that are very powerful for you? As you expand the number of stakeholders who will benefit and the size of their benefits, you will create a powerful momentum that will further speed your progress. If you would like to understand more about why this occurs, please see Part Three of our book, *The Ultimate Competitive Advantage* (Berrett-Koehler 2003).

Questions to help your organization identify the opportunities for identifying nth-degree opportunities through new measurements.

If you do not yet have nth-degree opportunity measurements in place, these questions will help you create those measurements. If you do have such measurements, you can use these questions to improve upon what you are doing today.

1. Which stakeholders (including end users, customers, opinion leaders, regulators, suppliers, distributors, partners, employees, shareholders, lenders, and the communities you serve) are or could be most critical to expanding your success to much higher levels?

Make this list as long as possible. Each group or person you identify should then be included in your new nth degree measurements.

2. How could each person or group expand profitable demand for your products and services in ways that would not be as helpful for your current and potential competitors?

Re-ask yourself this question as often as possible. Chances are that you are not considering enough ways to cooperate with your stakeholders. Also, as conditions and preferences change, new opportunities will open up to you. The answers to this question are essential building blocks to the type of measurements you need.

3. What's the best way to find out more about the capability of each stakeholder to help you expand profitable demand for your products and services?

For large organizations, the answer is often to measure their successes in the past that relate to your particular needs. The answer might mean learning how rapidly a given distributor has usually gained ideal distribution for products and services like yours.

For large groups of individuals like end users, the answer is often to measure their responsiveness to various marketing and performance choices you offer or could offer through market research. In doing so, be sure to segment groups of individuals into those who offer various degrees of potential profitability and speed of adoption. Then when you focus on the results for those who will provide the most profit and adopt the soonest, you will know better where to start your focus.

As you consider a stakeholder or stakeholder group, be sure to also look into the indirect effects of gaining their support. For instance, some early adopters of new products and services are also sources of great word-of-mouth influence. Some early adopters will tell hundreds of people about their positive experiences and influence early trial among those who admire the early adopter. In this way, focusing on early adopters who are also influential with others can greatly speed your progress.

4. What new forms of information can help you gain insights into nth degree potential?

For a mining company, creating a more helpful form of information might mean translating geological information into a three dimensional computer model that geologists could use to help identify where the most valuable ore veins are likely to be located. For a biotechnology company, this approach could possibly mean defining likely characteristics of genes that could be adjusted to provide patentable health benefits. For a chemical company, this opportunity identification measurement could mean identifying potential product characteristics that will enhance customer performance in powerful ways.

5. How can you compile what you have learned so that it can be more effectively shared with other stakeholders and experts who can help you devise new methods of capturing nth degree benefits?

Many stakeholders can only help in one dimension of nth degree elasticity. In such cases, they will be overwhelmed and confused if you provide everything you have learned. Instead, you will need to package the results of your measurements in ways that provide simple clarity in one or a few dimensions. We suggest that you consider creating strategy maps for this purpose. To learn more about this process, we suggest that you read *Strategy Maps* (Harvard Business School Press, 2003) by Robert Kaplan and David Norton.

Chapter 6

Step Two: Decide What New Measures Are Needed

The material in this chapter expands upon pages 149-162 in *The 2,000 Percent Solution*.

Having used the questions in chapter 5 to find nth degree opportunities for the future, it's time to return to the five best ways to grasp the opportunity you selected. So far in the workbook, you have been encouraged to expand your thinking and to be open minded about what you considered doing. Beginning with this chapter, you will be doing the opposite: Taking a critical look to find out what's practical...and what's not.

You could fill many shelves with business books that report how new strategic directions fail because those in the organization did not understand the new direction and lacked either the skills or the resources to create the new direction. Using your existing measurements and adding new ones can help you overcome these difficult problems.

In thinking about new measurements, you need information that helps you explore opportunities that interest you as well as information that helps you test your ideas about what could work. We'll look first at measurements that can help you explore the opportunities you have identified.

To make this chapter easier to understand, we will continue with the publishing example from chapter 4. As you recall, nth degree thinking identified achieving rapid positive word-of-mouth comments as what the publisher wants to optimize. The following six complementary methods for accomplishing that result were identified:

– Publish books written by well-regarded celebrities with intriguing new information

– Authors dedicate royalties to popular charities which will promote the books

– Companies donate books as part of their product promotions due to the subject matter

– Tie the book launch timing to a series of related broad-scale media events

– Create an appealing corporate-sponsored contest related to the theme of the book

– Provide newsworthy disclosures daily related to the book.

Let's concentrate on just the first item on this list to develop an example of what measures are needed. Feel free to add your own ideas to this example to enrich your understanding of this process. We selected a publishing example for you because we knew that our readers would all have some familiarity with what it takes to attract readers to a book.

First, it would be very helpful to know what influential book reviewers would like to read about and from what prominent authors. Book reviewers receive advance copies months before the publication date, and early reviews often help influential readers decide which books they want to read. In addition, book reviewers often informally tout new books that they like to their friends which gets the word-of-mouth process off to a fast start.

Second, we want to ask the same question to those who are eager to read and talk about books just as soon as they come out…and who have influence on a large number of other readers who also like to read books just after they come out (let's call them "early influencers").

Third, we would like to know what sources help these early influencers rely on to decide what books to read. We can then use that information to get the word out.

Fourth, we want to know what hints about the book's contents these early influencers are most likely to be responsive to. That information will help shape the book's design and publicity.

Fifth, we can benefit from finding out what nuggets of desirable information in the book would cause early influencers to send out e-mails and make telephone calls to share good news about the book.

Sixth, we can gain by finding out if early influencers want to see authors talking about their books. If yes, we need to define the venues where the early influencers are and would like to attend an author event.

Seventh, we will make faster progress when we explore the second through the sixth perspectives with those who make their decisions to buy and read books primarily from what the early influencers report (let's call them "early readers").

Eighth, we also want to build from the celebrity's fame and influence. To do this, the second through the sixth dimensions should be measured for those who are the most avid and easily stimulated fans for that celebrity and who also purchase or read books.

Ninth, we should also use the book's contents to identify those who are extremely interested in that subject, whether or not they are fixated on a particular celebrity. Again, the second through sixth perspectives should be captured for those who are book purchasers or readers.

Tenth, what other groups can you think of who would likely be early book purchasers or readers?

For those who would like more examples of this thinking process, we recommend *Crossing the Chasm*, revised edition (HarperBusiness, 2002). That book is focused on technology examples.

Questions to help your organization use new measurements to identify the best opportunities for implementing nth degree opportunities.

Implementation measurements are usually so finely tuned that it takes time to put them into place. As a result, it's unlikely that you will have these measurements before exploring a particular aspect of an nth degree opportunity.

For that reason, you should use the following questions to help you identify as many helpful measurements as you can. With that perspective, you can do a better job of informing those who will make the measurements what you need to know. With good design, you may find that the full extent of your measurements can be made at only a moderately greater cost than performing an incomplete set of measurements. Here is an area where you should plan to sleep on your answers before concluding that you are done with this section.

1. What types of customers will be most interested in your nth degree opportunity?

If you have very few potential customers, feel free to identify them individually. If you have many potential customers, pick some method of describing how they are different from those who will be not as interested. In the publishing example, book reviewers who are interested in the celebrity and subject were one such category.

2. What types of the most interested customers will be most profitable to attract in the beginning?

These groups should be from among those you identified in question 1. In the publishing example, you will probably agree that the early influencers group is the most profitable both because they will be buying the books early and because they will be influencing a lot of other people to buy books.

3. What factors that you can influence will be most important in attracting these most interested and profitable customers?

In the publishing example, these factors included the identity of the celebrity and the new information being presented in the book. Undoubtedly, other factors will also be important. The new measures should identify what all of the important factors are. If you have ideas about what these factors are, be sure to write them down so that they are tested in the measurement process.

4. What other groups of relatively profitable customers will be impressed by positive experiences among those identified in question 2 with your nth degree opportunity offering?

In the publishing example, these customers are those who pay attention to the views of the early influencers and those who write the earliest book reviews. In other industries (especially for industrial goods and services), customers are skeptical of those who have employed something in other industries. But there are exceptions, particularly in the other industry is well known to have high standards or difficult requirements. It's critical that your early successes be able to widen the market's appreciation for what you offer.

5. What factors will be most influential with those you identified in question 4?

In our publishing example, factors could include specific examples of the new information that is not revealed in the marketing and publicity literature and the enthusiasm of the comments made by the early influencers and book reviewers. In another case, factors that relate to the credibility of who said what and what they said will often be important. For instance, a single endorsement of your nth degree opportunity offering from a highly admired executive at a highly admired company will carry a lot more weight than a hundred endorsements from unknowns at companies that people feel are failing. If your offering has definable performance parameters, information about what the performance has been in comparable situations that are important to the customer can be critical.

6. Assuming that you attract those you identified in question 4, what relatively profitable groups of current and potential customers will those customers help you attract?

In the publishing example, these next most attractive and available customers will be the early readers, the people who pay attention to what those who are influenced by the early influencers have to say about new books they have read.

7. What factors will be most influential with those you identified in question 6?

In the publishing example, you may find that these later readers pay attention to a variety of variables beyond what their influencers have to say. These other factors may include how well displayed the book is in libraries and book stores, the word of mouth they hear from those the early readers do not normally rely on for book recommendations and how well the book is doing on best seller lists.

8. How do the interests of and influences on the averagely profitable customers vary from those you identified in questions 4 and 6?

Celebrity appearances involving autographing, handshaking and talks might be a big swing factor for many of these customers in the publishing example. It is critical to know about these differences so that your marketing activities will include the right activities at the right time. Otherwise, you will have a strong reaction from those who are highly profitable…but will fail to ignite the mass market which will provide the bulk of your profits. For more on this subject, we recommend *Crossing the Chasm* (*ibid*) as well.

9. Will any of these target customers provide you with inexpensive opportunities to test your offering with them before it is finalized?

Publishers and authors often circulate draft copies of books to get feedback from those who are representative of the market they want to serve. In high technology, customers are often provided with free "beta" copies of software and hardware to help both the company make adjustments and to demonstrate the superiority of the new offering to what has been available before.

Chapter 7

Step Three: Identify the Future Best Practice and Measure It

The material in this chapter expands upon pages 163-177 in *The 2,000 Percent Solution*.

You should now begin using the measurements that you identified in chapter 6. Use those measurements to estimate the most effective way that your current and potential competitors will be pursuing the nth degree opportunity that you identified in chapter 4 by using the implementation choices you uncovered in chapter 5. In looking for the answers, stay open to identifying other possible opportunities and implementation choices that will work even better.

The future best practice often isn't much more than a few percentage points of improvement over the current best practice. Why should you bother to identify the future best practice for such a small potential gain? First, the current best practice is often several hundred percent better than the average current practice. So the gap to the future best practice may be wide from where you are today unless you already are the industry leader in these dimensions. Second, you probably haven't looked at this perspective before in the context of the best nth degree opportunity, and positive surprises are likely. Checking will help you avoid shooting too low with goals for your new approaches. Third, thinking about the future best practice is a helpful context for seeing unexpected opportunities well beyond what the future best practice is.

It's hard enough to find out what the current best practice is. How can we hope to know what the future best practice will be? Obviously, no one can be sure....but you can learn important lessons even if your conclusions are wrong in detail.

How should you proceed? A good starting point is to locate the current best practice. You can often find the current best practice by simply looking at outstanding successes by competitors and reading articles about what those competitors and their customers say in print that the companies do well. You can find out more from those who know the competitors well. Possible information sources including former employees who have been gone for a few years and suppliers who have not been sworn to secrecy. Naturally, you should follow good ethical standards in your research and not mislead anyone about what you are trying to learn. In addition, you can interview relevant customers and other key stakeholders to find out how they perceive the best practice offerings and how those offerings are provided. In some cases, you can even become a customer of the competitors and directly experience what they do.

Once you know the best that competitors do now, shift your attention to what developments they are working on. These developments are often hinted at in financial reports, press releases, stories in various technical, trade and business publications, talks at conferences and in advertising to fill new positions. From such sources, you can get a sense of what size commitments are involved in the developments, what the proposed targets and deadlines are, and what progress has been made so far.

Independent of those investigations into competitors' plans and progress, look at the rate of improvement that competitors have typically achieved. Once you have measured that rate of historical progress you can project its continuation into the future.

What if you have potential competitors who are more capable than current competitors? Many companies do. Focus on those potential competitors who could bring some important new advantage to the industry. Such innovators are often start ups led by seasoned executives with innovation experience. Also watch out for are those who are very strong in other industries who could easily transfer those strengths into your industry.

You should also consider if you are threatened by new government programs that are advancing public domain capabilities (such as new technologies) that could be applied against you as well as new organizations that are pooling essential resources in new ways.

If you are in an industry that is affected by technology, be sure to also be on the watch for new patents and technical standards that could provide large advances for some companies as compared to others.

Applying these thoughts to our publishing example, the publisher should look at both what traditional publishers are doing with celebrities and new trends in how agents, impresarios, producers and other creative intermediaries are changing their relationships and contracts with the celebrities. Since Viacom is a powerful force in television, motion pictures, cable programming and books, the publisher should consider how Viacom could combine its resources and relationships in new ways to create the future best practice. In the process, the publisher should consider what advantages could be gain by teaming with Viacom as a partner to pursue 2,000 percent solutions.

Questions to help your organization identify the future best practices for implementing your nth degree opportunities.

Most companies have limited competitive information beyond what is regularly published by other companies in their financial reports, industry tracking services and occasional measurements in marketing research studies. Investigating the future best practice involves some additional data development as well as analysis of new circumstances that are affecting or could potentially affect your industry.

1. For the ways you want to implement your nth degree opportunity, which competitor does each aspect of that approach best?

In answering this question, feel free to break down performance into bits and pieces that could be combined in more effective ways by partners, suppliers or those providing outsourced services.

In the publishing example, the publisher could begin by finding out which celebrity books and publications have done the best which had a connection to a well-regarded nonprofit organization. This search should include how it was done in different categories. For example, Peter Drucker played a role in creating a nonprofit organization that originally bore his name, The Peter F. Drucker Foundation for Nonprofit Management. That organization was folded into a new organization, The Leader to Leader Institute, that continues to benefit from ties to Professor Drucker as well as his brand-name appeal to many authors, professors and business executives. Although business books are not such a large category in the industry, there may be best practices there that will apply broadly to trade books and novels by celebrities. Ms. Oprah Winfrey has also played a defining role in influencing the sales of books through her television show and magazine. Other lessons can be drawn from that example. Actor Paul Newman created a nonprofit company to benefit children and has written books to promote that charity as well as the products the company makes. Yet other lessons can be garnered from that example. Surely, other examples will occur to the publisher and to you.

2. What improvements have each of these competitors made in the last several years in the most effective aspects of what they do?

Your purpose in answering this question is to identify information to use in estimating how fast future improvements might follow. Be sure to gather information about when these improvements were made and how long it took to develop the improvements.

3. What improvements in their most effective activities are these competitors known to be working on?

Be sure to look for both improvements in the current best practice methods and in related methods that could advance best practice performance.

4. When is it likely that these improvements will reach the marketplace?

In drawing your conclusions, consider how long experts estimate that it would take them to achieve the new results, the speed that the competitor has advanced in the past and any public hints you can find of progress along the way. Be especially vigilant about looking for tests in progress that you can monitor.

5. Which potentially effective competitors seem to be planning to enter against you in the next five years?

Be sure to track announcements of new partnerships, new contracts, new hiring and new tests that might tell you something about the potential competitors' intentions.

6. When might these new competitors begin making their offerings?

Here, you are better advised to look for the earliest date rather than the most probable date. That's important because putting forward your innovations before the new entrant does will be a more effective way to compete.

7. Which start-ups and new ventures could become effective best practice competitors during the next five to ten years?

Almost every industry has conferences at which companies describe what they are working on and what their prospects are for the future. You would do well to visit those conferences as well as any trade shows where such companies would be telling future customers about what the companies are working on. In addition, check any other public sources of information you can find about these companies.

8. When could these start-ups and new ventures first reach best practice effectiveness?

In particular, you should think about which customers will be most attracted by these new forms of effectiveness.

9. What new technologies and industry standards are being developed that could change the future best practices?

Be sure to consider technologies and industry standards aimed at suppliers, distributors, customers and end users as well as those that will directly affect you and your competitors.

10. When will the best practices brought about by new technologies and changed industry standards first reach customers?

If the new technologies and industry standards are being developed in part by those who are not your competitors and your company is a potential customer, you can probably find out all you need to know through technical discussions.

11. What best practice improvement areas are not being pursued by anyone with the resources required to succeed?

These gaps in new developments are potentially rich areas for your organization to consider, particularly if you can conceive of a rapid and relatively low cost way to make progress in those areas. In our publishing example, the lack of a focus on publishers developing projects and then looking for the talent to execute them is an example. Television shows and motion pictures have always been developed that way. Why should publishing projects be any different? By drawing on the skills of those who are already familiar with the process, rapid progress should be possible.

Chapter 8

Step Four: Implement Beyond the Future Best Practice

The material in this chapter expands upon pages 178-186 in *The 2,000 Percent Solution*.

There's a simple solution for any mistakes you made in underestimating future best practices in your work based on chapter 7: Set aggressive targets well beyond what anyone else can achieve in the immediate future…and have excellent plans for implementing those targets. As long as you don't start living in a fantasy world with your new targets, you have little to lose in this regard. However, if you do get carried away with targets, morale will soon droop. A good method for taking the risk out of such aggressive targets is to ease your way in stages towards your ultimate targets. A great strategy will design the first improvement stage to cut off the most important strategic options for your most effective competitors.

Gillette in 2004 provides an excellent example for how this can be done. Without advance fanfare, the company switched its new products strategy for shaving. For a number of years, the company had advanced by adding an additional blade ….and then made adjustments to the combination of blades to provide a better shave. When the improvements were running of out steam in creating better shaves with the current number of blades, Gillette added another blade. In the process, Gillette went from one to three blades for its razors. Based on past timing, around 2004 or 2005 looked like when Gillette would go from three blades to four.

Consumers were obviously beginning to wonder where all this would lead. Would there be 23 blades someday? That didn't seem likely. The current path wouldn't continue forever.

Undeterred, Schick made a tremendous commitment to four-bladed razor technology and succeeded in beating Gillette to market with its product. In the past, Schick had almost always lagged Gillette in offering the next blade combination or improvement.

Imagine the chagrin at Schick, however, when Gillette announced instead the first electric wet shaver that looked like a hand shaver while employing conventional three-blade technology. How could Schick hope to compete? Well, it couldn't. It will take Schick a long time to match the new Gillette offering, and sales of four-bladed razors have been modest.

Note that by pioneering this new approach to shaving, Gillette will have new skills and knowledge that would allow it to push this new technology into four bladed shaving if it wanted to…or to make four-bladed shaving unnecessary as it did. Gillette's new M3Power shaver is thus an excellent example of implementing beyond the future best practice with a first stage advance that cut down on key competitors' opportunities for new products.

Schick's consternation must have increased when Gillette next introduced its Fusion shaving system in 2005 that features five blades that are closer together in both power and non-power versions.

The sources of new future best practices are many. But the easiest choices are often to add one valuable new element to something that already works as the best practice. Adding vibrating power to a wet shaver allows the blades to work more efficiently to set up and cut off whiskers than if you simply drag the razor across the stubble. The new Gillette shaver is an excellent example of this principle of adding just one new element at a time.

The Gillette idea is pretty obvious in retrospect. Electric shavers with rapidly moving blades have been around for decades. Recently, some companies had even begun offering electric shavers that were waterproof and allowed the person to use shaving cream without making a mess of the shaver. Naturally, it's easier to implement vibrating head changes to a make a traditional razor more like an electric than the reverse. Voila! You have a fine innovation.

Another way to move beyond the future best practice is to simplify products or services so they have fewer elements, have a narrower use and can be sold at a lower price. Small portable vacuum cleaners for cars were such an innovation beyond the future best practice in their time. Prior to these handy gadgets being available, you had to feed lots of quarters into oversized industrial vacuums at many car washes. The car wash vacuums were not very convenient and were inevitably very dirty. You needed a car wash for yourself when you were done. The small car vacuums quickly paid for themselves by reducing the cost of do-it-yourself at car washes or paying a car wash to vacuum your car. In addition, you had a more convenient way to vacuum so your car stayed cleaner…and so did you!

Extending beyond the future best practice need not be a new product. You can simply solve a problem for customers or end users. FedEx pioneered the use of tracking on its overnight envelopes and packages. A nervous customer could see where a critical package was and share that information with the person waiting for the package. If the package was delayed, the customer was able to document for the addressee that the shipper had done his or her part. Credibility rose for customers, their customers and naturally for FedEx. Before long, tracking became a common feature for shipping, and this feature was no longer an advantaged practice.

Advancing past the future best practice can merely call for the direct approach. In underdeveloped countries around the world, telephones are scarce. Public telephones are even harder to find. Making an international call can be quite a challenge, even if you can find a telephone. Into the breach came Gilat Satellite Networks, an Israeli company that developed a technology for beaming public telephone calls to and from communications satellite connections via fast, effective ground exchanges. Suddenly, great telephone service could be available anywhere a small satellite dish could be securely placed. Hundreds of billions in infrastructure investments are avoided while service is more speedily provided. Anywhere in the world you can now be in touch with anywhere else. Similar technology had long been used by the Israeli military. All Gilat had to do was to simplify the technology and make it cheaper for this new application to transform the world through improved communications.

The main requirement for passing the future best practice is to use your imagination to find ways to replace what is unnecessary, annoying, frustrating or otherwise undesirable. Good luck in your search!

Questions to help your organization surpass the future best practices for implementing your nth degree opportunities.

Many companies have little product, service or process development going on that looks beyond incremental improvements on current offerings. Yet such incremental improvements seldom yield advances beyond the future best practice. At the same time, those incremental improvements are often necessary to remain competitive in the meantime.

Customer innovation also presents some serious problems. Customers can articulate their problems with the products, services and processes in use today…but seldom can describe what they would prefer to replace those products, services and processes.

To help you overcome these substantial challenges, these questions should help you move the heart of the matter.

1. What is unnecessary in some circumstances about current offerings and processes?

Experience has shown that simplifying what is being done is often the easiest, fastest and least risky form of advancing beyond the future best practice. Also, customers can often tell you what is unnecessary if you describe the situations you want them to consider. For instance, experienced personal computer purchasers don't need to go to a physical store to try out what they are thinking about buying. They can specify their needs and would prefer to have a custom product that provides exceptional value because it doesn't have elements they don't want and need. Dell was able to make rapid progress using this insight in the personal computer market by combining its direct selling model with custom-built machines.

2. What is annoying in some circumstances about current offerings and processes?

Finding a product, a service or a process to be annoying creates an enormous desire within customers to replace those offerings and processes. By observing people using various offerings and processes, you can quickly perceive when such moments of annoyance occur, and can inquire to learn more about what the problems and potential solutions are.

Waiting in line is a problem that proves to be annoying in almost all situations. Innovations that eliminate lines or that make waiting in them more pleasant are often effective. Theme parks, for instance, now provide ways to ride the most popular rides with either no waiting or limited waiting.

Waiting to have products or services provided can cause similar annoyances. How can you provide what is wanted just when it is needed? Many suppliers do that now in a real time basis for their manufacturing customers.

3. What is frustrating in some circumstances about current offerings and processes?

People increasingly expect instant gratification. Finding something that frustrates them creates a double negative that prods them forward to pursue choices that provide the preferred, rapid results.

Almost no one wants to change a tire on a car. It's rare that the flat occurs in a safe, well-lit location on a dry, sunny day. In addition, the work is difficult to do without power tools…particularly if the lug bolts have been torqued on with a power tool. Jacks are typically flimsy and often require some peculiar adjustments. Unless you have used one recently, the jack may defy your understanding until you read the owner's manual. If you don't have an owner's manual, you are just out of luck.

Is it any wonder that people will pay a substantial premium for a tire that is hard to deflate? There are even some tires that you can drive for several dozen miles after they are flat. You can also buy products that temporarily re-inflate the tire for a few miles. In any of these cases, this means that you have fewer tire changing hassles. The friendly AAA person can then change the tire for you at home or work without any inconvenience.

The authors were impressed by this problem recently when a call to an AAA person for a tire change was countered with an offer to re-inflate the tire instead to see if it would hold air. Even AAA doesn't want to change tires if it can be avoided!

4. What is undesirable in some circumstances about current offerings and processes?

Some situations are so in-grained in our society that no one considers changing them. But they are certainly undesirable and could easily be improved.

Consider being a consumer who has to ship a heavy item. Whether you use the your postal service, UPS, an air cargo courier or a local packing store, you will have to take the item and properly place it into a package that meets shipping requirements…or you will have to cart the heavy item to a facility like a packing store that will do that packaging for you. Even if you do get help with the packing, the charge will often be more than the shipping for the goods. What's a consumer who needs to ship something heavy to do? The packing stores could overcome this problem by providing a pick-up service that would allow the consumer to hand off the problem where it lays heavily on their floor or shelf. Since such items are usually shipped during the day when pizza delivery people are often not busy, there's a pre-existing work force that could be added for this purpose.

5. What intensely desired improvements that solve problems identified in questions 1-4 can be made to the product, service or process that no one else is likely to be working on?

Your chances of success are improved if you can attempt to add more than one such improvement. In that way, if one of your innovations doesn't work or hasn't as much appeal as you hoped, you should still be able to move well ahead of the future best practice that would otherwise have occurred under a competitor's leadership.

6 Which of those improvements can be accomplished the fastest with the least cost?

Since you want to cut off the competition from the new path that you plan to lead the industry onto, you want to put in place first the innovations that leapfrog the competition the fastest. Then, you can layer on the more difficult, slower and most expensive adjustments late...and further extend your lead in advancing beyond the future best practice.

7. Which two of the fastest, least expensive improvements would be hardest for your competitors to quickly duplicate or improve upon?

Quick advances in the future best practice can backfire when a stronger competitor quickly follows with an improved version of your innovation. If none of your fast, inexpensive improvements can give you a lengthy lead time over your powerful competitors, you should instead choose improvements that are more expensive and time consuming...but do give you the necessary competitive insulation.

8. How can you involve new partners, suppliers, and other stakeholders to create the improvements you identified in question 7 faster and more effectively?

Effectiveness is the critical element here. Customers often don't notice...or worse...won't buy more from you because of the "improvements" they receive. If the change is effective enough in improving their value and perceptions of how they would like to be served, the likelihood of at least generating extra sales is greatly improved. Many companies fall down in their pursuit of the future best practice by aiming for improvements that are too small with resources that are too limited to be effective.

Chapter 9

Step Five: Identify the Theoretical Best Practice to Near Perfection

The material in this chapter expands upon pages 187-202 in *The 2,000 Percent Solution*.

The *theoretical best practice* sounds like something that can be hard to understand, identify and grasp. Since we wrote *The 2,000 Percent Solution*, we've switched from calling this object the *theoretical best practice* to calling the concept instead the *ideal best practice*. The *ideal best practice* seems easier for many people to think about. Feel free to use either term and to use the two terms interchangeably. Whatever you call the object of step five, look for how to deliver a product, service or process in the most effective and efficient way that it's every likely to be done.

You may find it helpful to understand the concept's origin. The concept of the *theoretical best practice* developed from listening to engineers describe limits they calculate for the efficiency of various materials and ways of these materials interact in chemical processes. Although it would be nice to have 100 percent efficiency in these chemical reactions, the potential is usually slightly below that level due to impurities and distribution inefficiencies in a container.

Interestingly, the potential for nearly 100 percent efficiency and effectiveness turns out to be available in many human interactions. Let's consider some nontechnical examples to help stretch your mind. Over many years of assisting executives who want to learn the eight step process, we've found that almost everyone agrees that communication isn't nearly as good as it should be in their organizations. So let's turn our attention to examples of near perfection that occur routinely in human communications.

When most people hear us talk about routine virtual perfection in human activities, they look very uncomfortable. But almost every human activity is performed almost flawlessly all of the time under some circumstances. Find out what those circumstances are, and you can begin to analyze what's missing from your situation. Add those missing elements, and you can routinely achieve virtual perfection.

Here's a communications example of routine perfection. People who have been in the military often cite the example of a platoon responding to the order to stand "at ease" with an immediate shift into the correct, more relaxed stance. It obviously took some training and practice to make that result come routinely and reliably, but most military veterans will tell you that their platoon had it mastered after just a few tries. Naturally, it didn't hurt the learning and execution that almost everyone prefers to stand "at ease" rather than "at attention".

People who have been in buildings that were on fire (like one of your co-authors) also report that the combination of flames, smoke and a fire alarm going off have a wonderful effect in encouraging everyone to leave the building in an organized way. One of the surprises that many people report is that individuals also look around to find those who are having trouble moving either due to physical limitations or emotional reactions to the emergency. Those same watchful individuals then take the initiative to be sure everyone gets out safely.

Why does responding to a building fire work so well? Naturally, everyone has been told and heard about the risks of fire from being burned, smoke inhalation and carbon monoxide poisoning. Everyone has also been through countless fire drills and has learned that it makes more sense to walk directly to the nearest safe exit without pushing and shoving. Appropriate exits are visibly marked and are easy to find. Also, as interesting as fires are to watch, most of us would prefer to watch from a safe distance. It's almost a natural instinct to move away. So the communication from the sounding fire alarm reinforced by evidence of a fire in such situations can create the correct actions virtually instantly.

In a track meet, the sprinters await the firing of a blank cartridge from an official's pistol to signal their start. Although some may leave early due to a desire for a fast start, no one who is uninjured will fail to leap from the starting blocks when the pistol sounds.

In some training sessions, those present have offered more than a hundred examples of near perfection in group communications. Can you think of examples where your organization does well now? Here's a hint: Do many employees fail to cash their paychecks?

What do these examples have in common? Here are some ideas to help you start answering that question. First, the communication is unambiguous. Second, the communication is hard to miss. Third, the listeners have a thorough under-

standing of what the communication means. Fourth, there is an important benefit for the listeners who pay attention and act promptly. Fifth, the listeners have
either been through the sequence many times before for real...or during practices. Sixth, the listeners have everything they need to act promptly.

Now, think about times when your organization's communications have
worked poorly. What was missing from among those six elements? In many cases,
there's little sense of an important benefit to the listener. In other cases, the communication is ambiguous or not even noticed. In lots of instances, listeners fail to
have the training and resources to be able to respond appropriately.

Where else does near perfection occur? Here are a few examples to help you
think about the subject. Almost every time you dial a telephone number from a
land-line telephone, you will be either connected to the right number or receive a
correct signal that the number you are calling is engaged. How many of the first
class letters you have sent failed to be delivered to the correct address? How often
does polio vaccine protect the person who receives it from polio in the first year
after the inoculation? How often have you bought a new car that didn't have four
well-inflated tires?

Questions to help your organization identify the theoretical (or ideal) best practices for implementing your nth degree opportunities.

We often fail to perceive the potential for near perfection. Why? People tend to take near perfection for granted when they experience it. From our work in helping executives grasp the theoretical or ideal best practices, we have become convinced that everyone has a vast reservoir of largely unconscious memories of near perfection being routinely accomplished by organizations. You can learn to draw on those experiences to inform yourself about what's missing from the nth degree opportunity methods that you identified earlier. Fill in those missing elements that made those experiences work so well by using the following questions, and you will soon have identified a valuable method for implementing your nth degree opportunity.

1. What information will you need to gather and understand to implement your nth degree opportunity in a nearly perfect way?

Look back at your answers from chapters 5-8 to help you compile this list. Add to the list any other elements that you now realize you need. If you are like most people, pursuing near perfection will change your measurement needs.

2. Where have you seen information developed like what you need now that was perfectly available, accurate and usable?

Here are a few examples of usually reliable information sources to get you started: library catalogues; stock price quotes from brokers over the Internet; e-Bay bid prices; new road maps; temperature readings on a thermometer; seeing the rain fall on your window; and the experience of tasting snow.

3. What elements were required for the information to be nearly perfect in the examples you developed for question 2 that are also necessary for your nth degree opportunity information to be perfectly available, accurate and usable?

Some possible elements could include direct experiences to test the information, a number of highly reliable cross-checks, a statistically valid sampling method, calibrated measuring devices that seldom fail, and skills in developing and interpreting the information.

4. How can you add those reliability elements you identified in question 3 to your information development?

In answering this question, for now put no limits on the expense involved. Later, you'll look at how to find the information in the least expensive way. But your thought process to find the least expensive way can only begin after you have found at least one effective solution…no matter how unrealistic its expense might seem to you now. Think of this thought process as being like an nth degree analysis of the opportunity to develop the information you need.

5. Who will need the necessary information?

In too many cases, powerful information is withheld from those who need it most. By thinking about who will need the information you have been designing, you increase the likelihood of finding a good solution and making the resulting information available to those who will use the information best.

6. When will they need the information?

Information is most helpful when received just before it's needed. If provided too early, it will be ignored or forgotten when decisions and actions need to be taken. Provide it too late, and people are misled by being under informed about what they should be doing.

7. In what forms will they need the information?

Not everyone is experienced with analyzing data. Format data in a way that the lessons are unmistakable, and the correct actions will be taken more often. If you ordered "relax" to a platoon instead of "at ease," the same uniform results would not follow.

8. What communications, training, resources and experience will be needed to use the information appropriately?

You may feel like you know how to read a thermometer and you probably do. But if you are used to the Celsius scale and suddenly are confronted with one in Fahrenheit (or the reverse), you won't quite know what the numbers mean unless you know how to convert from one scale to another. NASA learned this lesson the hard way when one set of engineers sent data in feet and those who received the data assumed the measures were in meters. An expensive Mars lander didn't make it safely to the red planet as a result of that confusion.

9. How can you use the increasing benefits of scale that are associated with networks to enhance the information you develop and use to identify the best theoretical practices for implementing your nth degree opportunity?

With network development and exploitation costs dropping rapidly, it often makes sense to involve more kinds of stakeholders and non-stakeholders to create new perspectives on what's possible. A good example can be found in the Goldcorp contest for geologists to find gold in the Red Lake mine that we describe in *The Ultimate Competitive Advantage* and in chapter 11 of this workbook.

Chapter 10

Step Six: Pursue the Theoretical Best Practice to Near Perfection

The material in this chapter expands upon pages 203-215 in *The 2,000 Percent Solution*.

After answering the questions, and gathering and absorbing the information described in chapter 9, you are now ready to look for the best ways for your organization to pursue reaching the *theoretical best practice*.

Let's consider climbing Mount Everest as a model for this task. Although Mount Everest has been climbed many times, there are still important strategic choices to be made about which path you want to use to ascend the world's highest peak. Almost everyone uses the same route, but there are alternative ones that are much more difficult. In fact, some of the possible routes have never been successfully completed. Even after you have chosen a path, you have other choices. Normally, climbers use the most modern equipment and are helped by lots of bearers who do most of the heavy lifting. In recent years, however, some climbers have chosen to go without supplementary oxygen and to use few supplies. After you have decided how to equip yourself, you have other choices to make about risk and difficulty. Many people have been injured or died when they continued to scale Everest while heavy weather was arriving that made the eventual descent too dangerous. Other choices await. People from many nations have never climbed Mount Everest before. Do you want to be part of a party that includes some of these people? Do you want to conduct innovative scientific experiments along the way?

Having made those strategic choices, you still have many tactical ones. How much training do you want to require everyone to have? What physical tests must climbers meet before they will join your expedition? Will you seek funding from those who will gain marketing value from the climb? Under what weather conditions will you start your ascent? Under what weather conditions will you scrub your planned climb? Will you reserve more than one climbing slot in a season to deal with the chance of inclement weather?

If you are not a mountain climber, those choices seem rather difficult to make. Let's assume, however, that you have all the information you need from the last chapter. Suddenly, the choices stand in stark contrast to one another with regard to one context: What is your goal?

For instance, if your goal is to make the fastest, most difficult ascent in world climbing history, your strategic and tactical choices will be much different than if your goal is to have the highest likelihood of finishing the climb and descending safely. Depending on your organization's skill, experience and resources, either goal could be an appropriate way to pursue the theoretical best practice. In fact, if your organization has never climbed Everest before, the latter goal might be a good interim step towards the former goal.

You should use a variety of tests to determine your choice of goal for pursuing the theoretical or ideal best practice and how you pursue that goal. Each test will tell you something that you need to know. If any test turns up a negative that cannot be overcome, you should abandon the direction that requires that you take on the negative factor.

Here's an example of what we mean by the goal tests. As you answer these questions, think about which goals could have negative consequences and which ones would not.

What's the minimum accomplishment required to create a lasting competitive advantage from implementing a solution nearing the theoretical best practice? If your company provides a form of climbing gear, you not only need to have it be used on a successful climb up Mount Everest, you also need for the gear to make a difference in achieving an uncommon result that others will respect. So your goal will have to include some way of demonstrating that your gear takes climbing to a higher level. If you make safety gear, you might have a series of planned safety tests during the climb to simulate problems climbers often have…even if your expedition doesn't actually have those problems.

What's the minimum accomplishment necessary to make the required impression on current and potential customers? We once interviewed a senior executive for a jet aircraft engine maker. He said that airline customers were very impressed if an engine on a plane taking off could ingest a Canadian goose without causing the engine to fail. That was the ultimate test at that time. In the mountain climbing world, such a test for safety equipment might be to have all other safety equipment fail, yet have the climber survive a dangerous fall and reach the summit.

What's the minimum accomplishment to prepare to set a higher standard with a subsequent effort? Every organization practices with something that isn't too hard in order to build the teamwork and skill to do the ultimately most difficult task well. In setting the stages towards the goal, each stage has to take you to a higher plateau much like each stage of a rocket launches you into a higher altitude from which the remaining rockets can kick you still higher.

What's the minimum accomplishment to create enough resources to permit continuing to approach the theoretical best practice? If each step is too tiny, the organization and its stakeholders will lose interest. Ultimately, such a series of efforts will falter even if progress is as intended. For example, if Lindbergh had flown across the Atlantic with a back-up pilot in case he got too tired or became incapacitated, his successful solo flight might not have created the same public sensation that pushed transatlantic flying forward.

What setbacks would be permanently fatal to your pursuit towards the theoretical best practice? A setback could be financial such as eliminating the funds to go forward. Other setbacks are psychological. For example, if you found yourself harming young children despite your best efforts, you might be so disheartened that you would not want to proceed. Other setbacks might include incurring a very negative public reaction or hostile legislation.

Questions to help your organization rapidly approach the theoretical (or ideal) best practices for implementing your nth degree opportunities.

Organizations are too easily satisfied. Leaders will gladly seek incremental opportunities to improve by 10-40 percent when they could improve by thousands of percent…even when the larger improvements are easier to make than the smaller ones. As a result, the theoretical best practice is seldom seriously challenged. These questions are designed to help you overcome that harmful bias.

1. Which alternative routes to the nth degree opportunity allow you to make the most improvement in the least amount of time?

In answering this question, it makes sense to use a variety of time lengths to see how the results you can expect differ. Some opportunities might not bear any fruit for four years, while others could produce enormous progress within a year. If the efforts are all affordable, it may make sense to pursue more than one of these choices. In that way, some of the fast paths can be yielding benefits while you continue to work carefully on longer paths that have a higher potential.

2. What are the most dangerous risks that must be avoided in pursing any alternative?

In answering this question, consider each current and potential stakeholder separately. Use nth degree thinking to assume that the rapid paths to progress you identified in question 1 fail in the most negative and harmful ways.

3. How can the paths to progress be adjusted to eliminate these risks?

Dealing with an unprecedented emergency situation can expose everyone to danger. Preparation for the same emergency when it is anticipated can turn the response into a routine and safe one. For instance, the first time you swim two hundred yards to save someone without training, you may find your own life at risk as the person grabs on to you and you lack the skill and endurance to respond appropriately. With life saving training, conditioning and experience, you would know how to approach and deal with the person so that risk is minimized, if not eliminated, even if the person is larger and stronger.

4. How can what is difficult for your organization to do be made simple, quick and easy by getting help from other organizations or stakeholders?

We all tend to back off when faced with something we haven't done before, even if the task isn't a particularly hard one. Rather than be daunted, you would be better off turning those tasks over to those for whom the tasks will be easy to accomplish.

5. What results will create vast enthusiasm and support for your approach to the theoretical best practice?

Going back to the Mount Everest example, if you found a way that almost any mountain climber could reach the top of the world's highest mountain safely at a cost that was much less than buying the average new car, you would have revolutionized the sport of mountain climbing. Undoubtedly, more people would take up the sport, and your equipment would be the talk of all those who like to exercise and enjoy adventure. What's the equivalent accomplishment in your industry?

6. What goal can you set that will energize your organization the most and give you a smooth pathway to approach the theoretical best practice?

In *The 2,000 Percent Solution* we gave the example of President John F. Kennedy setting the goal to send a man to the moon and return him safely before the end of the 1960s decade. Can you find an even more energizing goal than that for your organization?

7. How can you make achieving that goal seem likely to be reached in the minds of your stakeholders?

Without careful thought and communication, approaching the theoretical best practice can seem like "The Impossible Dream" which will keep people from pursuing the opportunity seriously. If you cannot find any other way around the credibility issue, you should consider how you can set a credible interim objective instead that will help you eventually reach your ultimate goal.

Chapter 11

Step Seven: Identify the Right People and Provide the Right Motivation

The material in this chapter expands upon pages 217-229 in *The 2,000 Percent Solution*.

If you want to set a world record, it's hard to imagine doing so with less than the best people in that field of activity. A key challenge, though, is to know who the best people are for doing something that no one has ever accomplished. But even if you have the best people, you may not succeed unless they make their best and most appropriate efforts. And money doesn't solve all the problems. Professional sports teams are familiar with the problem of hiring a top athlete at a record salary only to see the athlete's performance deteriorate because of being distracted by the new-found wealth.

In this part of the workbook, we will share some more advanced ways of making progress in these key activities and areas that will help you extend beyond what you learned in *The 2,000 Percent Solution*. We will continue to consider climbing Mount Everest as our example. We've now chosen our goal, which is to demonstrate the superior climbing experience and safety of a new concept in climbing equipment that our organization is developing. That equipment does not yet exist.

What talents do we need to find among the people who are involved in our approach to the theoretical best practice? The simple answer is that in the beginning we really don't know. New, improved concepts are often developed by those who have no familiarity with the particular industry but have a strong knowledge base in another field or context that can be applied. How do we proceed in taking different perspectives into consideration?

Most organizations will take a stab at defining the best way to implement the nth degree opportunity and go ahead with their best judgment about how to proceed to find the right people and encourage the right motivation. That approach is a serious mistake. Instead, we encourage you to get the whole world involved.

Here are some ways that organizations have drawn on worldwide resources to solve specific problems. As you consider your attempt to approach the theoretical best practice, consider how these approaches could be adapted to your situation.

Habitat for Humanity International (Habitat) is one of the largest home builders in the world. The organization is a nonprofit organized to provide low-cost, decent housing to those who could not otherwise afford it. The organization serves this purpose as a Christian ministry, but provides its benefits to people of all faiths. Habitat involves affiliates from every part of the world in pursuing its mission. Each affiliate shares knowledge and financial resources with every other affiliate so that global learning is enhanced. Knowledgeable home builders and crafts people donate their time to the organization, and train those who volunteer to help but have no experience. In the process, the organization has constantly improved its training of neophytes as well as its home designs. As a result, the organization can prosper by simply engaging the willing hearts and minds of almost all those who want to help their needy neighbors. By engaging so many people from so many different backgrounds, Habitat has been able to capture insights from both experts and newcomers whose hearts are inspired to do the best possible job.

Although the Habitat innovation model is a relatively slow way to make progress at the start, that model develops a momentum and energy that eventually takes its achievements beyond what one can normally expect from a highly successful profit-driven organization.

How did Habitat begin? One experiment was run in Georgia to see what might be done to help poor people help themselves. The land and building materials were donated, and volunteers were gathered from the vicinity to assist future home owners with the construction. Having succeeded with that effort, the founders realized that this approach could be even more valuable in underdeveloped countries because the needs are greater, costs are lower and volunteer help is more available. Implementation problems would be different in the developing world so more learning was needed. So Mr. Millard and Ms. Linda Fuller moved to Africa and ran the second experiment there. Having succeeded with those two experiments over many years, Habitat next focused on engaging more people and resources behind the organization's purpose.

What kind of people did Habitat need to begin pursuing the theoretical best practice? Habitat simply required volunteers who could ask for donations, find other volunteers and direct ordinary people to do the rest. They needed the right mix of skills to run an experiment with minimal resources. Interestingly, that's what's needed in almost any attempt to pursue the theoretical best practice.

Goldcorp approached a different problem of involving the whole world in its pursuit of the nth degree opportunity. The company owned some of the richest gold reserves in the world in its Red Lake mine. These reserves were found under land that had been mined for decades. How much untapped potential was left? That was unclear. he company's main limitation was the amount of capital it could afford to spend to locate and develop new reserves. How could it proceed to create a 2,000 percent solution for this opportunity?

The company's CEO took an unusual approach. He first invested in creating a three-dimensional computer model that captured all the exploration results the company had obtained for the mine. This model showed where the highest grade ore had been found. An imaginative person could then connect these pieces of data to make estimates about where veins of high grade ore might also be found in areas that had not yet been explored. Since much of the lowest part of the mine had not as developed as the rest, such new finds would probably occur at the bottom levels of the main shaft and possibly even lower. Peering at the new visual displays, his staff geologists immediately noticed many previously unconsidered high potential prospects. Most leaders would have simply said: Go ahead with those prospects.

Goldcorp took a different approach. The company put all of the computer model results into an Internet database where it was available to anyone. Geologists were invited to then submit ideas for locating new gold reserves through applying their knowledge to this information. Contest entry was free, and the submissions were reviewed by an independent panel of expert geologists who would award substantial cash prizes. At that time, gold prices were at a low compared to recent years, and there wasn't much work for many independent geologists. So many geologists saw the contest as a possible way to win valuable recognition at no cost in lost revenue, whether or not they earned one of the cash prizes. Hundreds of submissions were received. In the process many new ideas were generated that led to finding hundreds of millions of dollars of new, soon-proven reserves. Yet the cost of the contest and the prizes was less than a few months of normal exploration costs. Other gold mining companies rushed to follow Goldcorp's direction, and this new method is now an established business model for inexpensively locating low cost mining reserves.

Notice that in both of these examples, a process of letting people try out their ideas substituted for simply trying to guess who the best people are to do a difficult task that has not been accomplished before. Also notice that those involved in volunteering and in the contest were probably more motivated to do well by the psychological and emotional rewards they received by participating than the average expert is who works at full pay on a business-related problem.

How might these examples be applied to our Mount Everest example? Here are a few ideas we want to share to get your thinking started. You will probably have better ideas.

First, the Goldcorp contest could be adapted to define what should be tested using the new equipment. Everyone who does mountain climbs could have ideas about what sort of a test would prove superiority and would impress them to want to buy the new product. The winners could be selected based on how current and potential customers responded to the best suggestions as determined by an expert panel of judges. The winners could receive recognition through public relations activities and on the company's Web site.

Second, once the tests were determined through the contest, there could be another contest to define new design solutions to meet those tests. Methods to attract ideas could be added as well, such as those used in the toy industry to obtain new items from independent inventors.

Third, yet another contest could be offered to find other humanitarian benefits from the best of such design solutions. In this way, the gear would be designed to have more applications than just helping mountain climbers. Simple versions might help people navigate on icy sidewalks, drive through the snow more safely without tearing up the roads, and speed rescues in wintry conditions.

Fourth, the company could offer to provide a royalty from its new product sales for an existing nonprofit organization whose purpose closely tracks the benefits that the new products will provide. This would add another set of stakeholders who would support the company's new direction.

Fifth, the royalty-receiving nonprofit organization could then offer easier ways for people to learn how to use the new equipment at a moderate cost. For those with limited resources, some of the royalty money could be used to provide free equipment. The company could also make donations to assist in this process.

Sixth, the Mount Everest teams and tests could be set up so that several designs would be competing. This would create the potential for a television program to track the progress. The program could be done as a variation on the many National Geographic specials involving expeditions to exotic locales.

Seventh, the Mount Everest tests could then be repeated on other mountains and in other cold climates to see how well the gear works in different conditions than the extreme ones on Mount Everest.

Eighth, a new nonprofit organization could be developed to create new sports and popularize them by employing the new equipment. Paying sponsors could be found who would underwrite the cost of applying this new knowledge for children.

Questions to help your organization select the right people and motivation to rapidly approach the theoretical (or ideal) best practices for implementing your nth degree opportunities.

Organizations usually stop looking for the best people long before they have found enough capable candidates. Even with good candidates, organizations have a hard time figuring out who will perform the best. Yet, no organization can afford to hire all of the potentially high performing candidates. At that point, most organizations tend to use motivational methods that reflect traditional stalled thinking rather than pursuing the theoretical best practice to help people motivate themselves.

1. How can you expand your pool of people who might be able to help you by making what you need them to do easier?

When you read about the Habitat and Goldcorp examples, you probably noticed that both organizations began to making it easier for people to help the organizations. Habitat ran experiments to find better ways to build and teach volunteers to help. Goldcorp created the computer model to make the information easier to use.

2. How can you assist those who do help you be more productive?

In most cases, performance lags due to misunderstandings about what needs to be done, insufficient training, missing tools and resources, and poor coordination of efforts. In considering your nth degree opportunity, where can you easily overcome those limitations?

3. How can you increase the number of people who will know about the opportunity to work with you?

Approaching the theoretical best practice is usually something that organizations do in secret—almost as though they were creating a critical military weapon. Yet experience suggests that better performance comes from simply letting more people try their hand at creating 2,000 percent solution implementations of nth degree opportunities and choosing among the best results. Because of this advantage of numbers over secrecy, you want to hold out your opportunity to the world…but seek to keep enough benefit from what you learn proprietary so that you don't undermine your success.

4. How can you design your initial experiments for developing the theoretical best practice so that you will attract more people who will want to offer their ideas to help you?

For every person who can directly help, there are many more who can suggest a potential solution to some part of what you need to do. In this way, adding more suggestions can contribute to providing enormous improvements.

One possible solution is to offer a variety of motivational benefits. For example, Habitat appeals to people who volunteer with the organization for many different reasons. The families who eventually purchase the homes they build are expected to help with the construction. That "sweat equity" is their down payment. Having the families help build provides multiple motivations that would not otherwise be possible. It gives the home owning families a sense of personal investment that the families would not have if they simply purchased or were given the homes. At the same time, many volunteers report that they feel very excited by meeting the people who will live in the home. Other volunteers simply want to make friends in a new community. Some plan to do volunteer work on a regular basis, and Habitat's emphasis on weekend building fits into their schedules. Some people want to do work on their own homes, and see Habitat as a way to practice on someone else's home and materials. Still others would like to find repair and home construction jobs, and use Habitat as a training ground for the necessary skills. The potential motivational benefits are virtually endless from the current structure. If Habitat simply hired people to do the building, however, the results would be enormously less both in terms of home building and in terms of motivation to help.

5. How can you secure a cost saving from your experimental design so that the experiments are paid for by spending less on something else you would normally do?

In the Goldcorp example, the firm was spending millions every year to take core samples that would potentially reveal valuable gold veins. Goldcorp was able to divert part of that money to develop better ideas about where the gold veins might be found. The cost of its experiments created no net increase in the exploration budget. Afterwards, the firm was able to be more productive in its exploratory drilling so that the permanent cost savings in avoiding failed samples have been many times the cost of the initial computer work and contest. Because gold production has increased due to more productive testing, exploration costs as a percentage of sales have also dropped.

6. How can you make the benefits of working on your experiments intensely interesting for those who are involved?

Doing something that fascinates people provides immense motivation. Novelty helps as well. Notice that in each example, people were asked to play new roles that they had not taken on before. In many cases, these new roles were ones that the people saw as better ones. For example, in Habitat home projects experienced plumbers aren't just plumbing. They are primarily teaching and leading non-plumbers to plumb. In those roles, the plumbers can develop new skills, meet people they normally wouldn't rub shoulders with, and receive a lot of recognition for their knowledge. The geologists who entered the Goldcorp contests found out how their work stacked up against others. People who were competitive or interested in personal development could see this as a chance to improve themselves by comparing their results to what others developed. For these people the contest was almost like a post-graduate course in geology against an applied problem.

7. How can your design of the experiments create advance interest in becoming involved in your work or in support of the fruits of that work?

Many Habitat volunteers report that they decided to become involved after a friend told them about the fun they had enjoyed at a building site. Many geologists entered the Goldcorp contests after hearing other geologists tell about the fun they were having working on the contest. In fact, the winning entry came after two firms of geologists started talking about how they could combine their respective skills in a new way for the contest while waiting in a client's office. Publicity helps, but it's even more important to have something very positive and intriguing to publicize.

8. How can the financial resources you have available for rewards be provided in flexible ways that match the precise desires of those you want to motivate?

Some people would always prefer the money, while others would solely want personal recognition. Many people are in between, and their motivations vary at different times and in varying circumstances. You should not assume that one type of motivation will perfectly fit everyone. Provide choices that people will be enthusiastic about.

Chapter 12

Step Eight: Repeat the First Seven Steps

The material in this chapter expands upon pages 231-239 in *The 2,000 Percent Solution*.

Repetition creates mastery…and is avoided like the plague by those who like novelty and dislike discipline…and by those who are easily distracted. Fondness for novelty and distractions keep many from repeating the eight step process. Experience has also taught us that the better the 2,000 percent solution you just created, the more likely you are to avoid repeating the process. What's your likely reason? You will want to spend more time squeezing every possible benefit from the new solution. When that shift in focus happens, creating a great 2,000 percent solution can be a horrible stall keeping you from replacing your 2,000 percent solution with a better one.

How can these success-induced stalls be avoided?

Let's consider other fields to estimate what might be achieved through repeating the first seven steps. Measurements, for example, can be great motivations to exceed the current best. For instance, in sports all kinds of statistics are kept. Athletes take great pride in exceeding their personal best efforts both in practice and in competition, and are really excited on those rare occasions when they can surpass all those who have gone before. How can this model be applied to repeating the eight-step process? A good start is to measure everything about the effectiveness of the process you used in creating your new 2,000 percent solution and the benefits that process provided. Be sure everyone in your organization is aware of those measures and knows how much career progress and recognition will be enjoyed by those who exceed those measures when the process if repeated.

Sports can provide another clue. Athletes spend a lot of time training to improve their skill and physical capacity. Some even spend hours daily in mental and psychological preparation. The best athletes find ways to make the training interesting and satisfying. Runners and cyclists may listen to their favorite music and vary their routes. They also receive rewards in terms of when and how often they are allowed to compete based on their success with training. Those opportunities to compete in turn influence how much recognition they can receive. Creating 2,000 percent solutions in an organization can provide a similar kind of training challenge and experience, particularly for those who are new to the organization or who feel under appreciated but capable.

Music adds other lessons. Although not every sound a talented musician makes is a pleasant one, most practice time finds them bathed in beautifully vibrating sound. Musicians usually respond more than most people to this stimulus which makes practicing a lot more appealing. How can repetitions of your eight step process bring similar pleasures? One possibility is to allow those working on the repeated process to upgrade their work environment to make it more appealing.

Painting similarly suggests that pleasant surroundings are important. Most painters will arrange to have a comfortable and spacious studio with the best possible indirect lighting. Many painters also employ models whose appearances interest them. For those who are visually stimulated, providing well lit, beautifully balanced views might be helpful for creating the next generation of 2,000 percent solutions.

Dancers usually practice in front of large mirrors so they can see how they look, as well as to monitor how well they are doing. Make progress in developing new 2,000 percent solutions similarly visible to those doing this work, and improvement can be speeded up by providing a more objective view of their own performance. One way to do this is to capture key lessons of the original 2,000 percent solution development process so that new people can understand what worked well and what did not during the last iteration of the first seven steps.

Motion picture productions provide still other clues. Most actors will tell you that they have little sense of how good a movie they just worked on is. That's because they do not know which takes the director will choose, how the takes will be edited and how well all the performances come together. You need the perspectives of the director and editors to get a good sense of how it's all going. A 2,000 percent solution team might find it helpful to ask someone to keep looking at the big picture to help them monitor how they are doing and to suggest new dimensions that could be explored.

In most fields, coaches and teachers make a big difference by reinforcing what is working well and discouraging what isn't. A 2,000 percent solution team could also benefit from having a variety of coaches who help the team improve. This coaching role can be a great help on even the first 2,000 percent solution if the coach is experienced in this activity. When the authors help their clients and students through the process, we are always impressed by how much simple suggestions can help.

Any group can easily wander off the right path, even when closely watched and encouraged by outsiders. A great antidote is to continually spend time with those who will be the primary beneficiaries of the future 2,000 percent solution. These contacts will help eliminate misunderstandings about what is needed and shifting away from the most productive benefits. This retesting of what benefits to provide is critical when it takes a long time to develop the new 2,000 percent solution. Stakeholder needs may have rapidly evolved in the meantime, and the team runs of the risk of solving an irrelevant or less relevant problem.

Although few organizations have chosen this path so far, many organizations could gain by having more than one team working simultaneously on creating the next 2,000 percent solution. With multiple teams involved, there will be a natural rivalry that will provide a further spur to progress. In addition, ideas from one team may be able to help another team when the various teams share their learning at the end of each step.

Inject a few of the original creators of a 2,000 percent solution onto future teams working on better solutions, and you may stimulate wiser progress. Such a balance of naiveté and experience could help create better results in the same way that championship sports teams seem to benefit from a combination of young, talented athletes being seasoned by working with savvy, grizzled veterans who know what it takes to succeed. You should be cautious in deciding how many original creators to involve. With too many (or the wrong original) creators, you will simply create a too conservative approach that may discourage the wild imaginations of the newcomers to the process. Much of what's thought to be impossible by the old hands isn't really. Unrestrained imagining is critical to tear down this misconception.

Questions to help your organization repeat the first seven steps of the process to create vastly improved 2,000 percent solutions.

Four major failure possibilities dog every potential creator of 2,000 percent solutions. The first possibility is to let the organization be bound by stalls than cannot be loosened. The second is to put off starting the eight step process. The third possibility is not completing the process. The fourth is not repeating the process. These questions will help you overcome the fourth risk of failure.

1. What is the ideal team for repeating the first seven steps in the process?

Begin by speaking with those who worked on the first 2,000 percent solution and those who are the beneficiaries of that solution. What aspects of the potential improvements were well developed and which ones work less well now? What perspectives and skills were missing from the first effort that should be added to the next one? What perspectives and skills will continue to be needed for the new effort?

If a team was not used the first time, this question will be easier to answer. If an excellent team was used, ways to involve people from different backgrounds in the next effort should be considered.

2. How can the team members be motivated to see the process to a successful end?

In many organizations, new initiatives are seldom finished. In those organizations, rarely does anyone experience any negative consequences by not finishing.

Positive motivation will probably work better than punishments to encourage completion. One of the best positive motivations can be to make the work very high profile. Have everyone in the organization know who is on the team and how the team is doing. That kind of visibility can help bring out the best in a team that thrives under pressure. If such pressure would be counterproductive, then keep the team low-key and use some other motivating method that the individuals involved prefer.

Shift the evaluation process for these individuals to include team performance and their contributions to making the team work more effectively.

Many development organizations report good results from offering one-time incentives tied to the eventual results that the team's solution generates.

3. How can the team be isolated from harmful distractions?

Put together a great 2,000 percent solution development team, and you have probably pooled a lot of your organization's best talent. While that approach is admirable, it can also lead to problems. How will everything else that needs doing get done while these talented people work on a 2,000 percent solution?

An important step is to be sure that other capable people and effective resources are available to replace the team members while they are working on the 2,000 percent solution project.

Certain management members are more likely than others to interfere with the team and its focus. A wise choice may be to compensate these management members for their ability to leave the team alone and find other ways to accomplish the usual tasks.

4. How can you ensure that timely progress will occur?

You want to provide a lot of latitude for creativity, but you also want to encourage timeliness. A great tool is to agree on mutually acceptable dates for reviewing progress. For example, a team should be able to make relatively fast work of step one: how to make measurement be understood as a more valuable resource for creating 2,000 percent solutions. A fairly early review date could be set. If that date isn't met with appropriate results, you can ask the team to evaluate what it needs to do to improve…and set another early date to review progress on the same step.

If you start to fall behind, also evaluate what the root cause of the delays are. It can be helpful to have journals in place where the team members describe their daily efforts and progress. These journals and talks with team members should help isolate the hurdles that need to be overcome.

5. How can you be sure the process you use is a better one than the last time?

At each stage in the process, it will be valuable to encourage the team to look for better ideas, to find new information and to consider alternatives ways that the organization has never used. There needs to be enough slack in the budget, resources and schedule to allow considerable preliminary exploration of different directions. Many improvements can only occur after having new experiences. That means the team needs to find out about possible experiences and have the time and budget to have those experiences.

6. What promises can you make to external stakeholders that will ensure that you repeat the first seven steps in a reasonable amount of time?

If you have customers, you might promise when a new benefit will be available. If you have partners, you could promise that a new resource will be added for them before a certain date. If you have public shareholders, you can promise that key performance ratios they favor will improve. If you are regulated by a governmental agency, you can agree to a date for meeting a standard that they are seeking.

In each case, you need to make your promise so that you have both the time to find the solution…and to successfully implement it. Obviously, you shouldn't put your organization at unnecessary risk of failure, but some of that risk may be necessary. For example, Alexander the Great's troops were often spurred on by the realization that they would likely die if they did not win the battle.

PART FOUR

Help Others Learn How to Create and Implement 2,000 Percent Solutions

Most organizations learn about 2,000 percent solutions when an individual picks up *The 2,000 Percent Solution* on their own and decides to work with the book. Many fine solutions are created by talented, determined individuals working alone in this way, tutored only by the book's questions. In other cases, individuals use the book while being our students, and they receive guidance and support from us in going through their initial 2,000 percent solution.

These successful process initiators often keep their first efforts invisible from their colleagues. They often work at night and on weekends away from the office. The first experience is a test of the process, and there's no reason to seek wider awareness. Stealth change is the easiest way to make rapid progress in most circumstances.

Few, however, of the organizations proceed beyond that initial 2,000 percent solution success. There are a number of reasons for this. The person who initially used the process may feel awkward about asking others to put forth the same amount of effort in their spare time. There may be a limited experience in the organization in successfully employing new problem solving methods which may make the successful initiator skeptical of encouraging others. Colleagues may have little interest in learning new things. People may already be very busy with other activities, and one more task could overload everyone so that less is accomplished.

Whatever the reason for not proceeding to add other creators of 2,000 percent solutions, those who know the process and would like to introduce it to others can learn a lot from our experiences.

In the final two chapters, we share with you simple, effective ways to introduce the key ideas. Following such effective contacts, your colleagues can decide how much the process appeals to them. For those who then want to proceed, this workbook will help guide them.

Even if you have many people reporting to you, we suggest that you begin introducing this process by recruiting a single person who is interested in new ideas and improvements...someone with boundless energy. After such a person has a good experience, then consider taking your colleagues' success public and involving someone else. When the natural enthusiasts have all been recruited, then consider introducing the opportunity to everyone else.

Chapter 13

Identify Values and Learning Styles and Adapt Your Assistance to Match

The material in this chapter is not covered in *The 2,000 Percent Solution*.

Anyone you help learn to create 2,000 percent solutions will have at least some values different from yours and may also have a learning style that is totally opposed to what you prefer. But those differences don't have to be a problem. In this chapter, we outline ways to identify and bridge those differences, and turn them into assets.

In creating 2,000 percent solutions be employing teams, most groups have had three additional problems that need to be remedied:

1. They misunderstood one another's objectives for the company and themselves.

2. They misunderstood one another's willingness to consider changes.

3. They misunderstood each person's reasons for reinforcing the status quo in the past.

These misunderstandings need to be eliminated before a team begins working on creating 2,000 percent solutions.

The best way to overcome these stalls is to have lengthy, respectful conversations to separate the reality from the misperceptions. If you are working with an individual, you can simply ask the other person to share her or his views and then share yours. After you have heard each other out, you should both take some time to think about what was said. Later, you need to sit down again to identify ways that you can help one another.

If you are working with a team, the alternative to so many one-on-one conversations is to have a third party perform this task. This person could be someone from another part of the organization, a human resources manager, or an outside facilitator with interviewing skills. The third party confidentially interviews each team member for at least an hour. Each person's answers are kept private from everyone else. The answers are, however, then compiled and paraphrased in a report that keeps the responses confidential and anonymous while informing the whole group. This report lets the team see what the group's views are and where the differences are before any work is done by the group to improve its effectiveness.

Here are some questions that we have found to be very helpful in these one-on-one conversations:

1. What are your organization's objectives?

2. What should your organization's objectives be?

3. What works best now in your organization and should not be changed?

4. What works poorly now and must be changed if progress is to occur in key areas?

5. Why haven't these poor performances been changed in the past?

6. What will need to happen for the causes of poor performance to be eliminated now?

7. What do you perceive are each influential person's views about the needed changes?

8. Why did you decide to come to work for this organization?

9. Why have you decided to stay?

10. On a great day at work, what happens to make it great for you?

11. What do you tell your family and friends that you like about your work?

12. On a bad day at work, what happens?

13. Where do you need help to avoid bad days?

14. What help do you need to avoid the bad days?

15. What values are most important to you?

16. Where does your organization not follow those values?

17. What's the best way for you to learn about a new subject?

18. What's the best way for you to work on a difficult task?

19. What's the best way for you to help someone else work on a problem?

20. What are your best skills?

21. What skills would you like to improve?

22. What do you personally want to accomplish by working on your solution?

Be sure to follow up with probing questions where the answer is either ambiguous or introduces important related topics. How far should you go? Use your judgment but keep asking until you are both clear on the questions and answers. Keep the discussion comfortable for both of you. The best way to do that is to listen carefully, respectfully and with obvious interest. Sometimes you will be surprised by people pouring out difficult personal problems that you didn't expect or know about. Be as patient, supportive and sympathetic as you can be when that occurs, or you will harm your relationship and your ability to pursue a 2,000 percent solution.

Many people will come across in such a conversation as lost and confused in their work life, and possibly in their personal life. If you find someone like that, a wonderful additional activity to pursue is to help them lay out the personal goals that they would like to pursue through working on the 2,000 percent solution. Goal-setting can often be accomplished by simply encouraging them to draft goals and offering to be a sounding board concerning those goals.

For a team, the follow up to the individual interviews requires a delicate touch. After presenting the summarized results identifying where different views exist, the third party needs to encourage a discussion concerning where differences need to be resolved. As that discussion begins, the person who conducted the interviews should describe and clarify the nature of the differences as precisely as possible and invite people to ask questions. At some point, one of the people who was interviewed will volunteer (without being asked) to repeat what they said in private in hopes of encouraging others to agree or disagree. This candor occurs either because the person doubts what others have said has been reported accurately or because they want to find out who agrees with them and who doesn't. Generally, enough other people chime in so that what is being reported becomes credible. After the summary results have become credible to those in the meeting, the discussion quickly turns to the question of "what are we going to differently now that we know this".

With that focus, you imply need a facilitator to be sure the discussion follows a constructive path and no confusion develops due to misunderstanding the summary. The remainder of the discussion should then turn to planning the needed changes.

In the work style answers, you can expect that a wide range of styles for learning and cooperation will emerge. Some people will like to discuss their way through issues. Others will want to see a lot of information first and think about what they have learned in private before having any discussions. It's also likely that some people will want to know how the group feels about what is being worked on before proceeding. Some individuals will want to get their hands dirty working on the problem and then chime in to discuss what they learned. Some people with planning experience may want to run simulations of the challenges that need to be overcome to help identify possible solutions that will work in a wide range of circumstances.

Whatever you learn about work styles, it's important that you shape the directions, instructions and process that these people pursue for creating the 2,000 percent solution in a way that captures everyone's preferred ways of operating. That may seem very cumbersome, and it is. But the improved results will make the effort more than worthwhile. You can speed progress by putting the interview information and your description of the process into all of these styles. When you create this customization, you will find the group will relax, be much more open with one another and you, and be much more highly motivated to take the next steps.

Questions to help you introduce the eight step process to others.

In the body of the chapter, we have included a large number of questions to help you understand the values and learning styles of those you are helping. Before you ask those questions, however, we have found that it helps to understand why you are taking this step. Otherwise, you can lose sight of what's important. These questions will help you clarify your own motivations and goals.

1. What benefits would you like your organization to gain from having more people learn and apply the eight step process?

Think this question from several perspectives. One is what improved performance you are hoping will follow. Another is how the work environment will change as a result of enhancing skill levels in this process. Yet another dimension is how your relationship with change with the people who will now have these skills. What will be your reaction to that changed relationship? For instance, you may be excited to see these people enjoy their work more. A final dimension may relate to some stakeholder benefit that is very important to you.

After you know what these benefits are, consider sharing the benefits that you hope will follow with those you are helping. That sharing will encourage them to take the task more seriously.

2. Why are gaining those benefits important to you?

The answers may relate to living your personal values, meeting goals you have set for yourself, keeping promises you've made, or reliving some aspect of your life that you enjoyed in the past such as when someone was a mentor to you.

Once again, you should share your reasons. In doing so, you will probably help those who are learning the process to get in touch with their own reasons for going forward.

3. What is your usual teaching style?

A lot of people are unaware of how they help others learn. Before becoming a 2,000 percent solution advisor, you need to understand how you would normally approach this task. Otherwise, you will simply take your usual approach…whether or not it will work well with those you are helping.

A good way to start answering the question is examine how you would have taught yourself this process if you had been advising yourself. Most of us teach in a style that mirrors our own learning style.

4. What are the strengths of your teaching style for the person or the team you will be working with?

By being aware of those strengths, you can avoid forgetting to emphasize them.

5. What problems will your teaching style create for those you are helping?

Compare your answers to question 3 in this section to the answers to questions 10-22 from the main discussion in this chapter. You should also check your perceptions by describing your teaching style to anyone you will be working with and asking them what problems that style will create for them.

6. How can you improve your teaching style to overcome those problems?

Once again, it's a good idea to both come up with your own ideas and to check out those ideas with each person you are helping.

Chapter 14

How to Mentor Those Who Are Mentoring Others

The material in this chapter is not covered in *The 2,000 Percent Solution*.

Many people find it hard to make the transition between being someone who helps others learn a process and becoming someone who trains and mentors other learning facilitators. The natural tendency is to treat both tasks as being the same.

The biggest risk when both tasks are treated in the same way is for the mentor who is mentoring others to take too much initiative. When you are directly working with an individual or a team creating a 2,000 percent solution, you want the individual or the team to be very active in coming up with facts and ideas, and testing their ideas about what they have learned. If you do the same in mentoring mentors, you will end up with mentors who will use their superior experience and role to take over the 2,000 percent solution process from those who should be developing and implementing the solutions. That result is usually worse than having no effort going on to create 2,000 percent solutions. Those who are supposed to be learning will learn little except that they must check everything out with their so-called mentor before going forward. They also develop a dislike for such an authoritarian process and will discourage its use in the future.

Let's step back from that problem and think a little about what an effective mentor should do. A mentor is there to provide process guidance and emotional support. A key rule of being a helpful mentor is to wait to be asked for advice before providing any. Otherwise, you turn a learning experience into an eager dependency. This risk is doubly great when you are mentoring mentors because they will model themselves on your behavior and will often treat those they are working with in an even more directive way.

Does that limited role for mentoring mentors mean that you cannot explain your experience with creating and implementing 2,000 percent solutions? No, but you need to be informational in response to queries rather than being in command.

If you are feeling uncomfortable now as you think about this mentoring mentors role, be aware of that discomfort. It may mean that your instincts are to be too involved for this role.

The most important decision in creating new mentors for 2,000 percent solution creators is to pick people who will be good in the task. Not many people will be. If you are like most executives, you will want to select people who have been remarkably skilled in working on 2,000 percent solutions. You will see them helping others to become equally skilled and effective. While that may occur, it often will not.

Instead, you should realize that you can always arrange for such skilled people to be available to speak with and assist those who are working on 2,000 percent solutions without having them be mentors. For instance, one person may have a terrific way of describing and explaining the benefits of adding more measurements to people who haven't had that experience. If that same person is also very aggressive in proposing solutions without being asked, you should avoid asking them to be a mentor. How can you continue to benefit from their insights? You might instead do a brief videotape of what you want to capture about their views and experience, and have those who are mentors play the videotape when appropriate for those they are helping.

The ideal mentor has been through the 2,000 percent solution process successfully. You want people who take greater pleasure in the successes of others than in their own successes. In a team, these are the people who provide the social glue that keeps the group running smoothly. If you look back on a successful 2,000 percent solution that was developed by a team, ask those on the team to tell you which team members were most supportive and helpful.

What will be the hardest tasks for these new mentors to take on? Undoubtedly, it will be the interviewing those they are supposed to help to establish a more effective approach. A good way to help the mentors learn is to simulate the experience before they start mentoring. You could alternate playing the roles of people whose attitudes and preferences vary a lot. If you know the people well with whom the mentor will be working, you could even attempt to simulate their attitudes, knowledge and personal styles. In this way, the mentor could practice dealing with those circumstances. After the simulation is over, the mentor you are helping can describe what problems he or she experienced, and you can add your own observations about how else those problems could have been addressed if the mentor asks for more help. Undoubtedly, such a discussion would also encourage the mentor to raise other questions, and you could share other parts of your own experience and observations that are relevant.

Mentors will vary in how much help they want. Some will want you to do too much. In those cases, you should express confidence in how they are doing and suggest the circumstances under which it would be appropriate for them to seek you out. In addition to any role playing you do, you should also meet with the person for an hour a week in the beginning to hear them describe how things are going. Ask questions to let them know you are interested and to probe for hidden problems they may not be aware of yet. As they and you develop confidence in their approach, you can make these sessions less frequent.

Some mentors will want to keep you away from what they are doing. That's great if everything is working, but not so great if they are not being effective. If someone avoids meeting with you, ask them to share more information than you normally would about how the process is going. These people may not know when they need help until after a mess has been created.

In any case, you want to see work in progress relating to those who are creating the 2,000 percent solutions, beginning with the results of the interviews. If the mentors meet with you before those interviews are reported to the group, you can help them ensure that they have understood and summarized the key points. You can also discuss the various ways that the information can be discussed within the group to avoid having people feel attacked or not welcome in the discussion. In such a session, raise your points through questions. Otherwise, you will simply be dictating how to do the work. Let the mentor make the final decision about the best way to proceed. Even if the approach stumbles, the mentor will remember the questions you raised and will probably switch tactics before too much harm is done.

Questions to Help You Mentor Those Who Are Mentoring Others

This is the final set of questions for you to answer. You may find that these questions stimulate other ideas of ways you can improve upon your process for creating 2,000 percent solutions. Be sure to write down any such new insights that you develop on your own. Turning those insights into questions will be more powerful in helping you than these questions will.

1. What were the most confusing parts of creating your first 2,000 percent solution?

Having become familiar with mentoring those who are creating 2,000 percent solutions, you will soon find yourself moving beyond the questions, concerns and fears that you had in the beginning of your mentoring experience. Chances are that those who will be mentoring others will have many of those same questions, concerns and fears. By discussing those areas, you are most likely to be a sympathetic mentor and to provide helpful ways to be a mentor for those who are new to the process. The result will be for those who are new to the process to move through the process faster, more effectively and more confidently.

2. Where did those you first mentored to create 2,000 percent solutions have the most problems?

Undoubtedly, some of those problems relate back to the unique characteristics of your organization, the challenges your organization faces and your own ways of mentoring. By being aware of those patterns, you can help new mentors to be more effective in these areas.

3. How can you help those you are mentoring to mentor others so that those they mentor can be more effective in these same areas?

A good way to introduce this subject is to describe your own experiences and ask those you are mentoring for suggestions about how you can be more effective. In many cases, they will see solutions that you didn't see in the past. In this way, some of those you are mentoring can help you be more successful in helping others of those you are mentoring. If other people in your organization are also playing the same role you are, be sure to seek out their advice and experience.

4. What are helpful signs that a 2,000 percent solution process is moving along successfully?

We suggest that you identify several such signs for each step in the process. By having spotted your own measures of successful progress, you will know what to look for as you select mentors and help them evaluate and improve progress.

5. Who will make good mentors for those who are new to 2,000 percent solution processes?

In listing your candidates, also consider how well these people will like the role, and who they would be particularly effective in helping to create a 2,000 percent solution.

6. How much time can each person spare to help with 2,000 percent solutions?

In addressing this question, you should also think about how they can free up more time to work in this area.

7. In what ways will each person need help to become a better mentor?

By identifying where mentors need more strength or skills, you can begin to plan ways to help them.

8. Who would those who are starting to create new 2,000 percent solutions most like to have as mentors?

Having a mentor you prefer can be a little like the effect of Dumbo's magic feather. You gain a lot of confidence that you will succeed and that the results will be worth the effort.

Afterword

Only you know the best way for you to apply this workbook. Because your answers to the questions in the workbook will change over time, you may find it helpful to fill out your answers anew each time that you either repeat the first seven steps to create a 2,000 percent solution, you mentor someone or a team working on a 2,000 percent solution, or mentor someone who is mentoring those working on 2,000 percent solutions. If you decide to re-ask and re-answer the workbook's questions, be sure to look at your former answers. Those answers will give you further clues as to where you need to focus.

For some, this will mean adding pages into the workbook. For others, a series of time sequential answers will appear beneath each question in the workbook. For those who write the most extensive answers, this may mean creating an electronic file with dated answers in it. Still others, having more than one copy of the workbook may be the easiest way to record answers over time.

Progress towards the theoretical or ideal best practice will vary a lot from organization to organization and from performance area to performance area. Many clients and students have created 2,000 percent solutions that put them five or ten years ahead of the future best practice without making much of a dent against the theoretical or ideal best practice. Others have immediately found 2,000 percent solutions that carved out a high percentage of the potential for moving towards the theoretical of ideal best practice. As your organization proceeds, you will want to carefully understand what your organization does when you achieve the latter that doesn't happen when you accomplish the former result. We hope you will share what you learn with us.

We deeply appreciate your commitment to and efforts on behalf of creating 2,000 percent solutions. You are remaking our world into a better place in a way that few other efforts can hope to match. Thank you!

2,000 Percent Solution Services

Certified tutors are available to assist you in using *The 2,000 Percent Solution* and *The 2,000 Percent Solution Workbook* to locate your stalls, overcome those stalls and create 2,000 percent solutions. These tutorials can be provided for individuals or groups, either on-line or in person.

Examples of outstanding papers written by graduate business students based on these materials can also be supplied to you by e-mail.

If you submit your 2,000 percent solution paper to us after you use this workbook, you may be eligible to join the 2,000 Percent Solution Club. New solutions are circulated among the members, and you will have chances to contact and share ideas with other members.

We also offer certification training in tutoring 2,000 percent solution students.

These materials and this training can be licensed by your organization to achieve even greater improvements.

The authors are available to give speeches and conduct workshops on these subjects.

Mitchell and Company also provides consulting services for creating and implementing 2,000 percent, 4 million percent and 16 billion percent solutions. These solutions can be applied to establish a new business, a new industry or make a giant leap ahead of your competitors.

For more information about these and our other services, call us at 781-647-4211, send an e-mail to ultimatecompetitiveadvantage@yahoo.com or write to us at Mitchell and Company, P.O. Box 302, Weston, Massachusetts 02493 USA.

Praise from Former and Current Graduate Business Students for Tutorials Based on The 2,000 Percent Solution *and* The 2,000 Percent Solution Workbook

"Professor Donald Mitchell brought me to a whole new world. I used the course based on *The 2,000 Percent Solution* and *The 2,000 Percent Solution Workbook* to establish a strikingly promising business strategy for my company, which other business courses failed to help me provide. Now I am doubling my company's business and profit very rapidly and realizing my dream: Exponential Business Success."

—Hiroshi Fukushi
President, FD Green Co., Ltd., Thailand; Managing Director, AET Manufacturing Co., Ltd., Thailand; and Director, Ajinomoto Co. Ltd., Thailand

"This course obliterated my complacency. Our business has turned the corner due to application of the 2,000 percent solution principle. No more 6% interest on medium risk financial investments—40% in 9 months, an annualized 755% improvement. The blinkers have gone."

—William Kempen
Partner, Impact Human Resources, South Africa

"Donald Mitchell's on-line tutorial alerted me to company stalls that must be avoided. It was very instructive to learn how not to do something. The creation of a 2,000 percent solution showed me that there are always better, cheaper and more effective ways to organize any business activity."

—Neil R. McGrath
CEO, Application Developers Pty. Ltd., Australia

'The 'Exponential Business Success' course is quite ideal for small entrepreneurs and those working for reputable organisations to create solutions to the many snags that retard an enterprise's exponential growth. The course is a powerful tool for those who are keen to bring significant change in their personal lives and organizations they work for.

"I am one of many students who have benefited greatly from this course. I am not only an effective member of my family and the organisation I work for but a visionary affiliate of my society as well.

"The author of the books *The 2,000 Percent Solution* and *The 2,000 Percent Solution Workbook*, Professor Donald Mitchell uses both resources to mentor his students in a more practical way. The first book takes the learner through *stalls, stall busters* commonly found in any organisation and the *eight steps towards creating a valuable business solution*…while *The 2,000 Percent Solution Workbook* guides the learner through a series of practical applications of the 2,000 Percent Solution process You do not need to go to class for the course is offered on-line."

—Jacob V. Yesaya
Senior Lecturer in Vocational Education, Department of Vocational Education and Training, Botswana

"This course enabled me to explore comprehensively all aspects of my organisation, ranging from the traditions we follow blindly, the complacency which had set in the way we serve our customers, the unnecessary bureaucracy and the blind spots in me and in my organization. This course helped me immensely in learning and acquiring expertise and know-how on how to manage and discipline my thinking, to be more creative, and build my self-confidence in my ability to make a big positive difference in other peoples' lives."

—Elijah Chingosho
Associate Professor, Rushmore University, Africa

"Under the wonderful guidance of my advisor, Professor Donald Mitchell, I developed goals, new habits and skills to achieve professional as well as personal success to lead a happy life."

—Burra Ramulu
Supervisor, SAFCO-3, Saudi Arabia

"When our effectiveness suffers because of stalled mind-sets, when our productivity is low, because we are stuck in bad habits that disfavour our projects, 2,000 percent solutions are effective answers. In his courses, Donald Mitchell shows students how to identify stalls and break through them by creating 2,000 percent solutions. I have found this idea of creating stall busters that supply exponential success highly useful in my professional and private life. Once people identify the main problems and create the 'right' solution to tackle them, not only do you solve the problem that you had in the first place, but you might also find yourself solving problems that you didn't think that you even had and get results that you never even thought you could achieve. Donald Mitchell's courses on the 2,000 percent solution are a highly beneficial lesson to any students who want to get things right and reach goals beyond their expectations."

—Oliver Haggenmuller
Executive, Switzerland

"I found Don Mitchell's 8-step process an excellent practical tool to demolish all hindering forces and barriers in my work. *The 2,000 Percent Solution* gave me insight to look far beyond the limitations of my present reality. His feedback was very precise in a way that pinpointed the key areas where the performance of my business could be dramatically improved."

—Roy Rissanen
MBA, Missionary Pilot, Africa

978-0-595-37488-5
0-595-37488-3